IMAGES
of America

St. Landry Parish

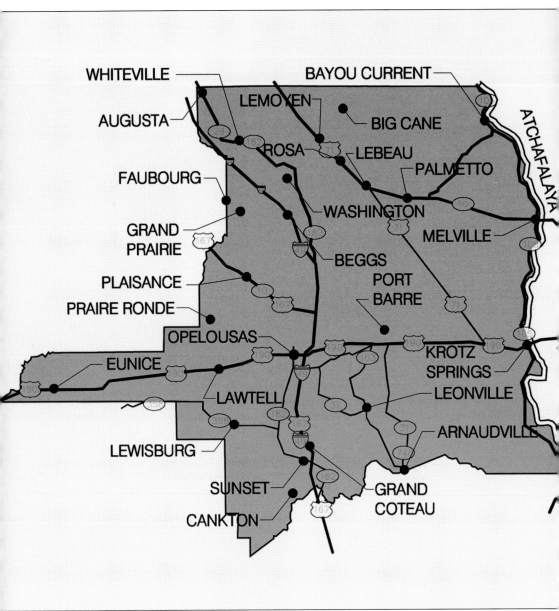

Over the past 300 years, waves of immigrants arrived in what is now St. Landry Parish, including people from France and Spain, Acadian exiles from Nova Scotia, Germans, Italians, Irish, and Asians, as well as English-speaking persons. This created a "cultural gumbo" in the parish. The Acadians' capacity to assimilate other cultures eventually gave birth to Cajun-Creole culture, a culture also influenced by African-Caribbean and Native American elements. As seen on this map, St. Landry's communities are named mainly for early settlers and local terrain. (Courtesy of Andrew Perrin.)

ON THE COVER: Marie Andrepont is shown driving a tractor in a parade in Opelousas in the 1920s. (Courtesy of the Acadian Museum.)

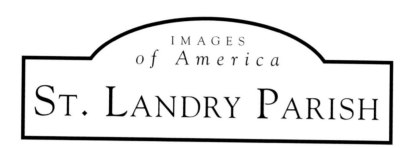

IMAGES
of America
ST. LANDRY PARISH

Philip Andrepont, Patrick Morrow,
and Warren A. Perrin

ARCADIA
PUBLISHING

Published by Arcadia Publishing
Charleston, South Carolina

Printed in the United States of America

Library of Congress Control Number: 2013935141

For all general information, please contact Arcadia Publishing:
Telephone 843-853-2070
Fax 843-853-0044
E-mail sales@arcadiapublishing.com
For customer service and orders:
Toll-Free 1-888-313-2665

Visit us on the Internet at www.arcadiapublishing.com

We, the authors, dedicate this book to our ancestors, who sought to pass on to their descendants their beautiful culture, which today has become threatened and, unfortunately, too often scarred by individuals who have exploited it for economic gain; to the courageous people across Acadiana who are working tirelessly to protect the integrity and beauty of our diverse cultures; and, finally, to our beloved spouses, Alice Morrow, Debby Andrepont, and Mary Perrin, who have given to us their support for this book and, more importantly, their love.

CONTENTS

ACKNOWLEDGMENTS

We were inspired to write this book by Hadley J. Castille, the late fiddler, who was never afraid to defend his heritage. According to retired judge Robert Brinkman, Castille had strong opinions against using the word "coonass," the insulting term levied against Acadians. Brinkman recalls: "[Castille] was playing at the Sierra Club in California and Pres. George H.W. Bush introduced himself and said 'Oh, you're one of those coonasses from Louisiana.' Hadley responded, 'Mr. President, I'm offended by that term.' Bush apologized and said he would never use it again."

In 1981, the Louisiana state senate passed a resolution condemning the use of "coonass." Sadly, today, the use of and profit from this offensive slur by some, including the song "RCA (Registered Coonass)" by Jamie Bergeron, reaffirms negative stereotypes and its vestiges of pre–civil rights racial discrimination. We, like Castille, condemn the use of this slur. To use the term is to dishonor our elders, who suffered to maintain our culture. The operative word here is respect—or lack thereof, by the offenders—for our forebears. Tellingly, on October 13, 2012, Louisiana secretary of state Tom Schedler announced a new policy that the state will no longer issue trademarks for the slur.

Responding to our pleas for assistance were Shane Bernard, PhD; Chris Dunbar; Vincent Darby; Betty Wolfe; Maynard Sanchez; Wayne Doucet; Tom Angers; Dr. Donald Pavy; Adele Pavy Comeaux; Judy Doucet; Marie Richard; Kaye Bernard; Gail Amy; Mona Siebert; E.A. Thistlewaite; Lanell Marks; John N. Harper; Cleo Cheuk; Richard Bordelon; Ann Savoy; Gabrielle Savoy; Geraldine Edrington; Mary Gale LaMonte Devillier; William Eaglin; David Simpson; Karen Lagrange; Alice Alden; Patrice Melnick; Judi Lucito; Tina Doucas; Howard Austin; Anya S. Burgess; Boisey Pitre; Angelle C. Lege; Rebecca Henry; Theresa Singleton; Carl Brasseaux, PhD; Chere Coen; André Comeaux; Rep. Raymond "LaLa" Lalonde; Louis Michot; Darrell Bourque, PhD; Christine Soileau; Stacey M. Schulze; Bob Casanova; Ida Pavy Boudreaux; Nolan Gobert; Carrol "K.K." Taylor; John Slaughter; Douglas Sandoz; Linda Doucet; Dr. Ladislas Lazaro III; Alice Carlin; Mark Majors; Leslie J. Schiff; "Sis" Laporte; Donovan Hudson; Donald Cravins; Morgan Goudeau III; Virval Bradley; Bishop Michael Jarrell; Myrina Foster; Herbert Brown; Keith and Ginger Myers; Amanda Fontenot; Marie Renaud; Juanita Wiltz; chef Paul Prudhomme; Bishop Dominic Carmon; J.A. Allen; Mavis Frugé; Dr. Barry Ancelet; Celeste Gomez; Andrew Guidroz; Ann Andrepont Gamble; Reggie Dupré; and Sen. Armand and Margaret Brinkhaus, who loaned us Ruth Fontenot's 1955 article "Some History of St. Landry Parish." Thanks to Stanford historian Dennis L. Bark, PhD, a senior fellow at the Hoover Institution, who allowed us to quote from his writings. We appreciate Sim Sandoz contributing his great-grandfather William J. Sandoz's 1925 article "A Brief History of St. Landry Parish."

Unless otherwise noted, all images appear courtesy of the Acadian Museum. Thanks to Darylin Barousse, who prepared the manuscript; André Andrepont, who documented the photographs; and Mary Perrin, who contributed her superb editing—including "brutal" comments.

—Patrick C. Morrow, Philip Andrepont, and Warren A. Perrin

INTRODUCTION

The early history of St. Landry Parish occurred not in a vacuum but in the context of colonial, national, and international history. In 1682, the French claimed Louisiana, including the region that would become St. Landry Parish, as a colony. Spain claimed the same region, viewing all of Louisiana west of the Mississippi River, including the Mexican province of Texas, as part of Mexico.

Into this disputed territory wandered some of the earliest settlers of St. Landry, including, for example, Joseph Le Kintrek dit Dupont, who, with his business partner, French adventurer Joseph Blanpain, traded horses, fur, and other goods with the Attakapas and Opelousas Indians. The latter people, about whom relatively little is known, gave their name to the Poste des Opelousas, also known as the Opelousas District. This place name referred to a region of south-central Louisiana made up today, more or less, by the modern parishes of St. Landry, Calcasieu, Cameron, Beauregard, Allen, Jefferson Davis, Evangeline, and Acadia. The current volume does not examine this entire multi-parish region, but rather only the area that, in 1910, after many changes in boundaries over a period of roughly a century, became modern-day St. Landry Parish.

While the aforementioned Joseph Blanpain ended his days in a Mexican prison after Spaniards captured him trading illegally with the Orcoquiza Indians of east Texas, Le Kintrek opened a trading post around 1750 at the spot where the fabled Bayou Teche sprang from its mother stream, Bayou Courtableau. Later a major St. Landry Parish trade route, Bayou Courtableau bore the name of Le Kintrek's son-in-law Jacques-Guillaume Courtableau, who in 1765 took ownership of some 8,000 acres bordering the Teche, the Courtableau, and the minor waterway Bayou Marie Croquant (now known as Bayou Little Teche), which emptied into the Teche about five miles east of present-day Opelousas. This made Courtableau one of the largest early landowners in the region.

Others followed Le Kintrek and Courtableau, including French immigrants, French Creoles (persons of French descent born in the colony), and Acadian exiles who spread out from initial settlements farther down the Teche. With these pioneers came Louisianans of African descent, both enslaved blacks and *gens de couleur libres*, or free persons of color. By the late Colonial period, this cultural blend would be reflected, for instance, in the muster rolls of the local militia. According to a 1777 list of Opelousas militiamen, the 109-man company included soldiers with French or French Creole names, like de la Morandiere, Soileau, and Fontenot; Acadian surnames, such as Jeansonne, Richard, Trahan, and Comeaux; and names with roots in other places, like Stelly, which is German.

Among these soldiers were no doubt a number of black Creoles, both enslaved and free; armed black militiamen were not uncommon at the Poste des Opelousas. Indeed, some of de la Morandiere's men bore surnames that suggest African heritage. At the very least, their descendants would possess a mixed-race African heritage. These surnames included, for example, Lemelle, Bello, Thery (Theiry), Carrière, and de la Fosse. When, in 1784, the Spanish naval explorer José Antonio de Evia ascended the Teche to hire or borrow local militiamen for a foray into hostile Indian territory, the commandant gave him, as Evia recorded, "twenty militiamen of Atacapàs and Opelousas . . . which well-armed could defend against the . . . Indians, if we are attacked." Those militiamen, Evia noted in Spanish, consisted entirely of "Negros, y Mulatos," or blacks and mulattos.

Anglo-Saxon and Scots-Irish settlers also began to make their way into the region that would become St. Landry Parish. Legendary Cajun musician Dennis McGee once famously noted that all McGees spoke French, thus implying the name had become ethnically French. McGee was right, because in the place from which he hailed, l'Anse des Rougeaux, near Eunice in St. Landry Parish, McGee *was* a French name because everyone there named McGee spoke French. Ultimately, however, the surname hailed from Scots-Irish roots, suggesting an English-speaking antecedent who, like so many others, settled in Cajun and Creole south Louisiana only to be swallowed up culturally by the French-speaking majority.

This changed dramatically in the 1900s, when Americanization led to the rapid decline of French speakers in St. Landry Parish and other Acadiana parishes. English became the dominant language, and, while French is still spoken in St. Landry, it has been joined by Spanish as increasing numbers of Hispanics immigrate to the parish, a trend reflected in the current format of KSLO radio in Opelousas.

There, at the station where my father, swamp pop musician Rod Bernard of Opelousas, played "Cajun swing" and country and western music in the late 1940s and spun "race records" (an early name for black rhythm and blues records) in the 1950s, the broadcasts are now entirely in Spanish. As the *Daily World* observed in December 2012, the station, "which used to broadcast local programming in both French and English for generations of local radio fans, has become Acadiana's first Spanish language radio station." St. Landry thus reflects changes occurring elsewhere in America at this time. Yet, St. Landry clearly remains proud of its history and culture, which stem from a frontier amalgam of French, French Creole, Acadian, Cajun, African, Indian, and other influences. In fact, it is this very blending process that accounts for the richness of St. Landry's distinctive history and culture.

—Shane K. Bernard

Holding degrees in English and history from the University of Louisiana at Lafayette and a PhD in history from Texas A&M University, Shane K. Bernard is the author of several books, including *The Cajuns: Americanization of a People* (2003) and *Cajuns and Their Acadian Ancestors: A Young Reader's History* (2008), which is now available in a French translation as *Les Cadiens et leurs ancêtres acadiens: l'histoire racontée aux jeunes* (2013). Bernard's paternal ancestors have lived in the St. Landry area since the time of the Poste des Opelousas.

One

ORIGINS

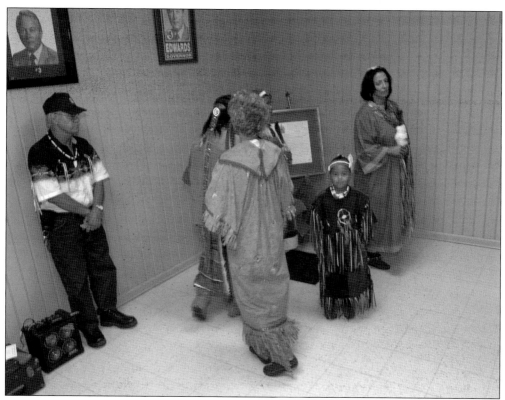

The prehistoric St. Landry inhabitants arrived in the region over 12,500 years ago in nomadic hunting groups. Archaeologists have identified 110 prehistoric dwelling sites within the parish, with three dating back to the Paleo-Indians of Louisiana, who lived in the area as early as 10,500 BC. This photograph shows Attakapas native people dancing in August 2012. The dancers are, from left to right, Theresa Semien Gobert, Francisca Nelson Gobert, Gloria Boxie, and Brandon Boxie. Chief Nolan Gobert (left) provides the music.

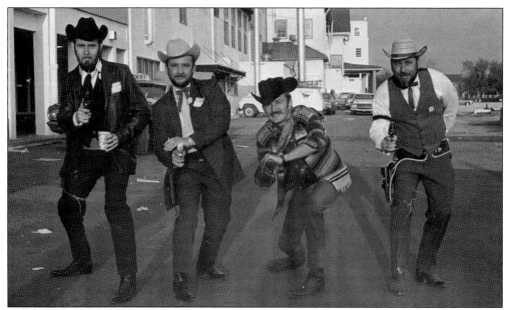

During the historic period (after 1500 AD), Attakapas Indians roamed the area of St. Landry Parish. One band, the Opelousas, eventually gained control of the land. The city of Opelousas, the seat of the parish, derived its name from this tribe. Here, from left to right, Paul Boagni, Allen Penick, Wayne Doucet, and Huey Bourque show off their costumes at the New Orleans Fairgrounds in 1976 while celebrating the 250th anniversary of the founding of Opelousas.

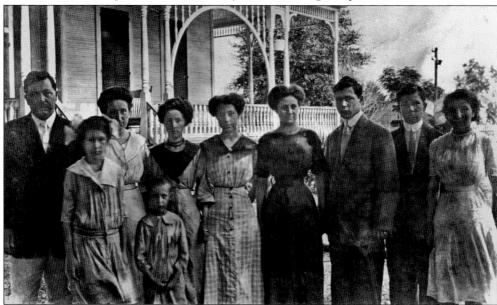

In 1519, Alonso Alvarez de Pineda explored the Gulf Coast. In 1682, Robert Cavelier Sieur de La Salle descended the Mississippi River, claiming the territory for France and naming it Louisiana. The Andrepont family is seen here in 1908. They are, from left to right, (first row) Marie Eva Andrepont and Victor Andrepont; (second row) Yves Andrepont, Anna Estelle Vidrine Andrepont, Blanche Marie Andrepont Decuir, Rose Marie Andrepont Dossman, Felicity Marie Andrepont Bordelon, Lawrence Andre Andrepont, Oscar Andrepont, and Stella Andrepont Major.

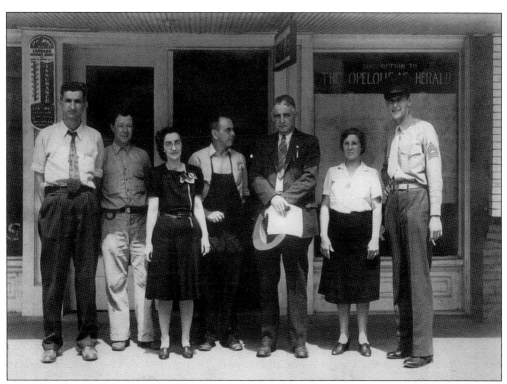

The French government of Louisiana
established the Poste des Opelousas in the
territory of the Opelousas Indians. The
post became a stopping point for travelers
going between Natchitoches and New
Orleans. Seen above in front of the offices
of the *Opelousas Herald* are, from left to
right, Sam "Lefty" Tarleton, Lawrence
Andrepont, Lillian Boudier, Bascoe Wyble,
Arthur Bernard Reed Sr., Marie Cahanin
Reed, and Arthur Bernard Reed Jr.

African slaves were brought to Louisiana
principally from Senegambia (West
Africa) and greatly influenced the culture,
language, and cuisine of the area. In 1724,
Louisiana institutionalized segregation
when it adopted the Code Noir (Black
Code), the paternalistic French and
Spanish laws governing relationships
between the races. Even though
interracial marriage was prohibited, a
group of mixed-race offspring of French
men and African women came into
being. Seen here in the late 1800s is
Francois "Nonc BeBe" Jolivette.

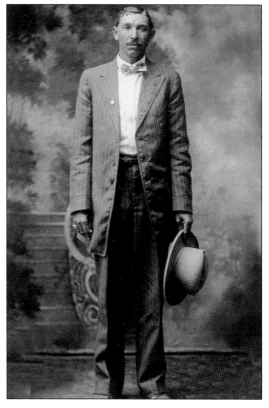

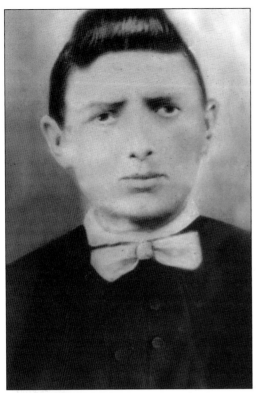

When Jean Joseph LeKintrek and Joseph Blanpain formed a partnership to trade with the Opelousas Indians in the 1740s, they settled in Opelousas with their three black slaves, who were the first Africans in the area. The Spanish government took over Louisiana in the 1760s and imposed their laws, known as Las Siete Partidas. Louisiana prospered under Spanish rule. In the late 1700s, Spanish settlers joined the French inhabitants of Opelousas. Seen here in 1905 is Georganna "Tant NaNa" Jolivette.

In about 1765, the Spanish built a military and trading post in Opelousas, and the old Indian village, now known as El Post de Opelousas, became the governing center of the entire southwestern part of Louisiana. Seen here is Amy Cormier, the director of public relations for the Louisiana Attakapas Opelousas Prairie Tribe, which now has three websites and a Facebook page. A petition will be filed with the state seeking official tribal recognition.

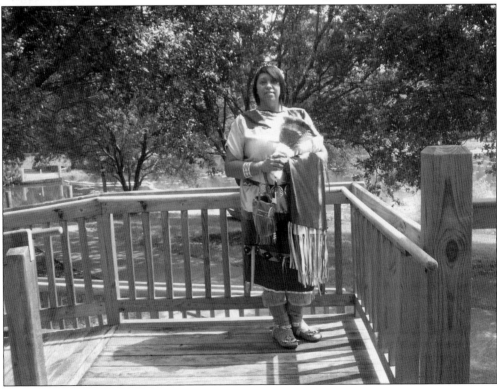

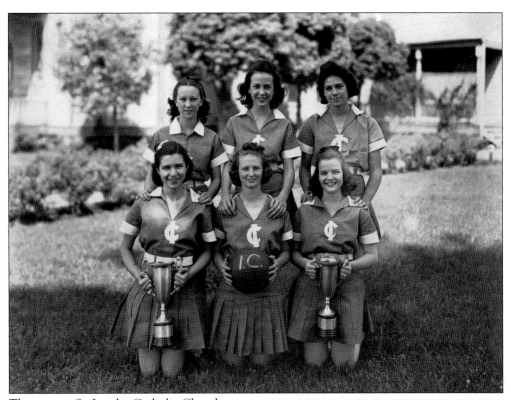

The present St. Landry Catholic Church building was constructed in 1908. The building sits on the same lot that was donated by Michel Prudhomme in 1798. The 1939 Catholic girls' basketball team pictured here included, from left to right, (first row) Ida Pavy Boudreaux, Dorothy Oge, and Bonnie Hollier Tilly; (second row) Helen Carriere Bordelon, Ruby Lawless, and June Voitier Cassanova. The team's coach was Louise Perry.

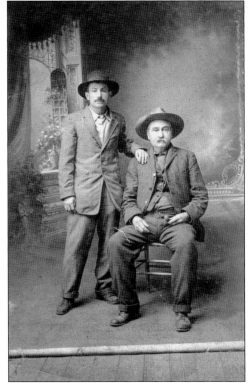

On April 4, 1768, Spanish governor Bernardo de Galvez issued an order that required the commandants in all of the Louisiana districts, including St. Landry, to prevent any arriving Acadians from settling in their posts. The Spanish wanted the Acadians to settle in areas that would provide some protection from the still-threatening Native Americans. The first Bertrands who settled in the Opelousas area came from Canada. By 1766, Amable Bertrand dit Beaulieu of Montreal was at the Opelousas Post. Seen here are Ozema Bertrand (left) and his father, Homer Bertrand, descendants of the pioneers.

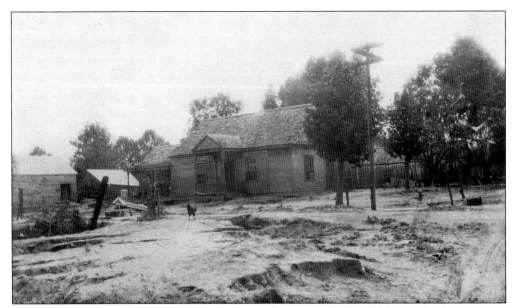

Because of flooding and termites, early settlers built houses on cypress blocks off of the ground, and, inside the walls, they put *bousillage*, an excellent insulating mixture of Spanish moss and mud. In 1927, the Atchafalaya levee broke at Melville, sending floodwaters throughout south Louisiana. This photograph shows some of the damage caused by the flood of 1927 in St. Landry Parish.

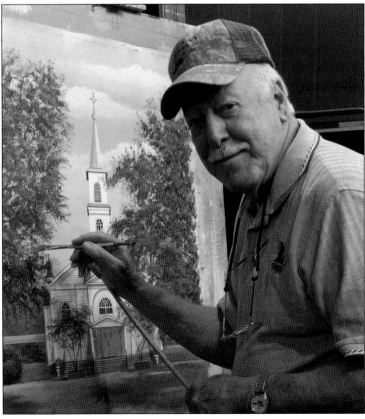

In 1769, Spanish governor Alejandro O'Reily ordered Capt. Don Eduardo Nugent and Lt. Don Juan Kelly to the districts of Attakapas, Opelousas, Nachitoches, and Rapides. Many settlers came to the region in the 1800s, including the Darby family. Seen here is Vincent Darby of Arnaudville, a self-taught artist who possesses the talent to see the beauty of south Louisiana and transpose it onto canvas in his own special way.

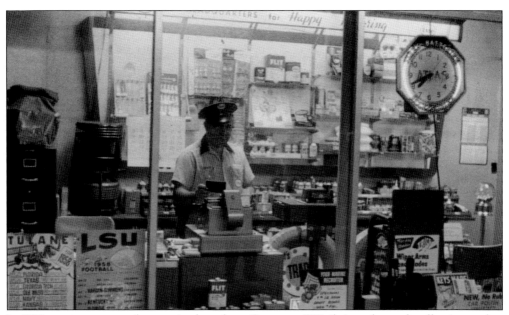

In 1770, to encourage settlements in the colony, Governor O'Reily issued an order allowing settlers to acquire Spanish land grants in the Opelousas District. In 1770, Jacques Bertrand, the second Bertrand to come from Montreal, settled in the Eunice area. Finally, three Bertrand families that had been exiled from Acadia entered Louisiana in 1785 with the migration of refugees from France. Seen here at his Esso gas station in 1958 is Aldus "Black" Bertrand, a descendant of the first Acadians in the region.

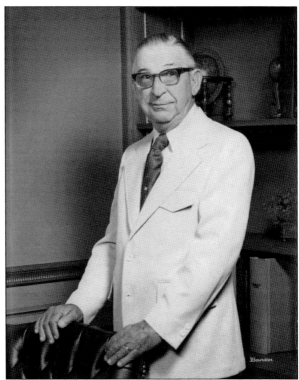

By the end of the 1700s, the French controlled the state once again, thus attracting Francophone settlers such as the Goudeau family. Morgan Goudeau Jr., seen here, was a civil engineer in St. Landry Parish who worked on most of the capital improvements in the parish from the 1930s through the 1970s. In the 1940s, he helped build the Thistlethwaite Boy Scout Camp, and was later awarded the coveted Red Hat by the Boy Scouts of America. Today, his grandson Chris Goudeau, an attorney, is the honorary consul general of France.

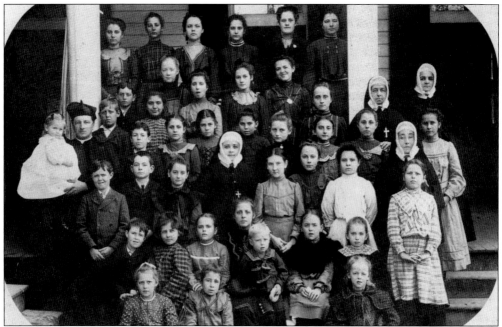

Established by a legislative act on April 10, 1805, St. Landry Parish was first called Opelousas County. Msgr. William Joseph Teurlings (left), who was named the pastor of Washington in 1898, is seen here at the Mount Carmel Sisters Convent holding an unidentified child in front of the school. In 1925, William J. Sandoz penned the article "A Brief History of St. Landry Parish," in which he stated, "St. Landry stands in the front rank of the country parishes in the matter of schools . . . excellent brick buildings have been constructed."

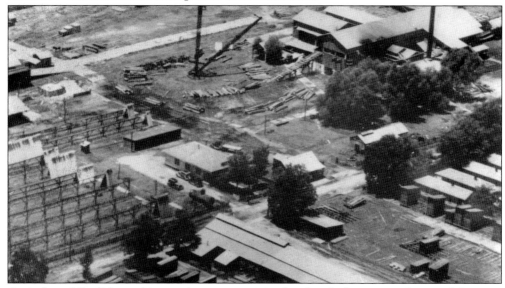

An influx of English-speaking settlers came to join the already diverse population of the area. Through the years, other groups arrived to settle in what became St. Landry Parish from places such as Germany, Italy, and Ireland. In 1906, Thistlethwaite Lumber Company was established in St. Landry Parish by John, Allotes, and Jesse Thistlethwaite under the direction of their father, Edward, of Indiana. In 1924, the company moved to Opelousas, where it operated until 1954.

Two

ACADIANS

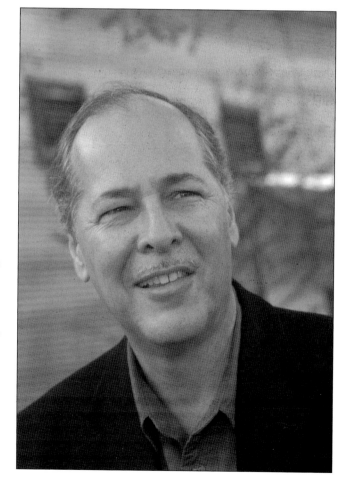

Beginning in 1755, Acadians were deported from Nova Scotia by the British en masse, in what was called le Grand Dérangement, or the Great Upheaval, to its colonies, where they were held for seven years. Since the Treaty of Paris in 1763 prevented them from returning to their lands, in 1764, some Acadians departed for places like Quebec, France, and Louisiana. Eunice native and award-winning filmmaker Pat Mire, seen here, documented their epic story in the 2000 film *Against the Tide*.

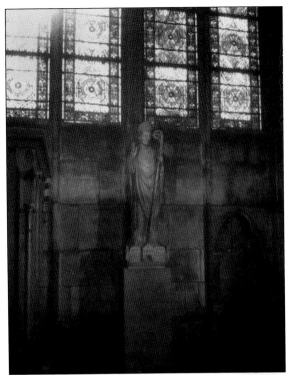

St. Landry Parish was named for the Catholic parish that was established about 1767 in the Opelousas Territory and named for Saint Landry, the bishop of Paris in the mid-650s, whose statue, seen here, is in Paris's Notre Dame Cathedral. In 1765, the first Acadians arrived in Louisiana, which was then owned by Spain. Officials welcomed them, and some settled in Opelousas. Their ancient French dialect is still an important part of the area's linguistic mosaic.

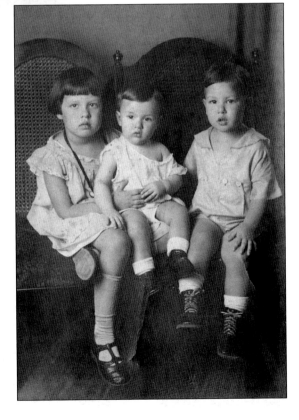

Unlike most Acadians, some who settled in St. Landry had not first been exiled to the British colonies. In 1755, many Acadians were captured by the British, but they managed to escape and fought an insurgency campaign until 1759, when Quebec fell. The leader of these militants was Joseph "Beausoleil" Broussard, who eventually led the first large group of Acadians, including the Boudreauxs, to Louisiana in 1765. Seen here from left to right are the Boudreaux children: Gladys Elise, Albert John, and Charles Adam.

Following the French and Indian War in 1763, the British viewed Acadians who had avoided deportation as threatening. Many had been imprisoned for three years on Georges Island in Halifax, Nova Scotia. Among the descendants of the French who settled New France in the 1600s, the ethnic Acadians' language transformed into a distinctive dialect now known in Louisiana as Cajun. Samuel "Sam" Guidry, seen here, was an Acadian who served in World War I as an interpreter in France.

In 1765, the Acadians who settled in the parish remained apart from others in the area. This reinforced their ethnicity and strengthened their new community. The first Guidry to settle in the Opelousas Territory was Pierre Guidry, of Acadia and Maryland. Before his death in 1825, he had acquired a fortune, including over 2,000 acres of land in the Grand Coteau area. The photograph below, taken in the early 1940s in downtown Cankton, again shows Sam Guidry, a farmer, school bus driver, and the operator of the People's Cotton Gin in Cankton.

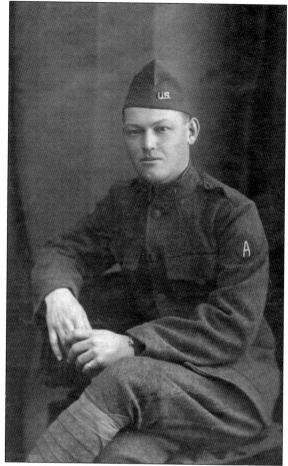

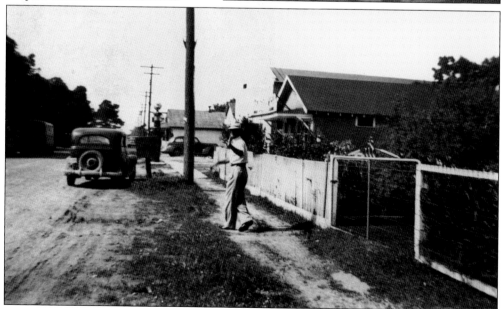

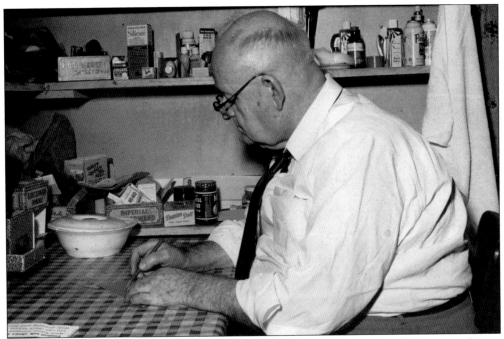

In the 1771 census, there were 10 Acadian families listed. Author Jean-Francois X. Mouhot, PhD, in his book *Les Acadiens réfugiés en France* (2009), deals with the Acadian refugees who were deported from the colonies in 1755 and who, after some time in France, migrated to Louisiana in 1785. Mouhot, a Georgetown professor, commented, "My long-standing interest for humanitarian action drove my initial interest for studying the measures by France to help the Acadian refugees." Seen here is Frank Penn Morrow, Arnaudville's first pharmacist and its mayor from 1929 to 1933.

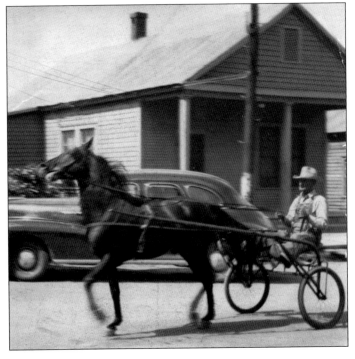

St. Landry Parish, incorporated in 1811, is situated in the heart of what is now called the French Triangle. The English term "Cajun" is a corruption of the French word Acadien, which describes the people who had been exiled by the British from Acadia. The most successful of the Cormier pioneers was Acadian-born Joseph Cormier and his sons Michel, Ancelet, and Joseph Jr. By 1788, they had 700 head of cattle in the Bellevue prairie, south of Opelousas. Anglais Cormier is seen here riding a one-horse sulky in Sunset.

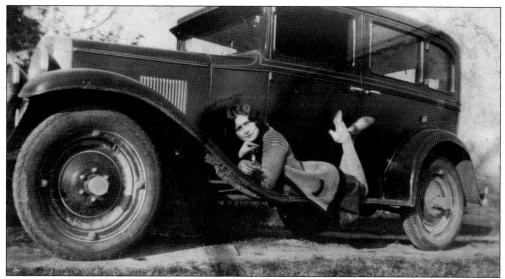

According to Stanford professor Dennis L. Bark, PhD, by the early 1800s, the Acadians represented three groups: a small number of wealthy planters, a middle class that included farmers, and a much larger class of farmers whose poverty limited their social mobility, leaving them little choice but to preserve their Acadian traditions. It was from this latter class that Cajuns emerged. By 1777, Pierre Savoie had settled on Bayou Mallet in Faquetaique Prairie. Here, Acadian Wilhelmina Guilbeau Savoie poses on a car's running board.

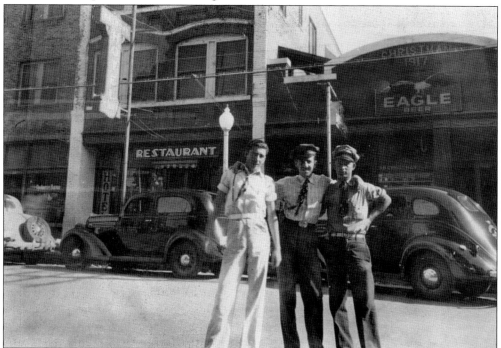

Between 1820 and 1860, the largest group of French immigrants to come to Louisiana were called the "Foreign French." About 550,000 of these skilled immigrant Francophones prospered because of their talents as carpenters, tradesmen, and shopkeepers. Seen here from left to right are Opelousas cabbies Wilbur Andrus, Gabe Hargroder, and Joe Graffagnino.

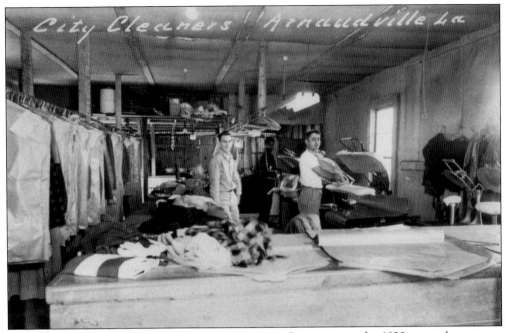

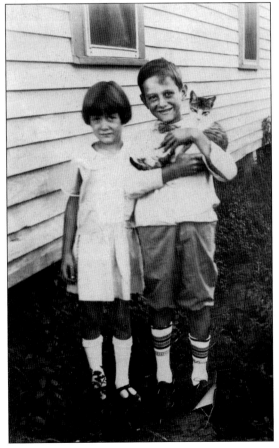

Beginning in the 1820s, resettlement to Louisiana by the "Foreign French" was caused by political instability in Europe, which stirred waves of migration. The immigrants, mostly craftsmen and small businessmen, became store owners, shoemakers, and mill workers. Seen here inside City Cleaners of Arnaudville are, from left to right, Edwin Darby, unidentified, and James Huval, the owner of City Cleaners and the mayor of Arnaudville.

At the end of the 1800s, having reached an accommodation with the natural resources, the descendants of early Acadians, along with settlers from Germany, Africa, England, Spain, Ireland, and Italy, were on the brink of a new period of sociocultural change. These diverse cultures came together to create a mélange of what is known today as the Cajun culture. Seen here in Opelousas in 1925 are Hazel Bernard and her brother Louis V. Bernard holding a cat. (Courtesy of the Louis V. Bernard Jr. collection.)

At the 1946 Yambilee festival, designed to promote the industry, the Cajun culture had advanced to such a degree that Cajun crafts, music, and storytelling were combined into a cultural festival involving children. The first Yambilee queen was Jean Horecky of Church Point. Ludo Pitre, a sweet potato farmer from Prairie Ronde, is seen here celebrating his birthday with his wife, Eva Bertrand Pitre.

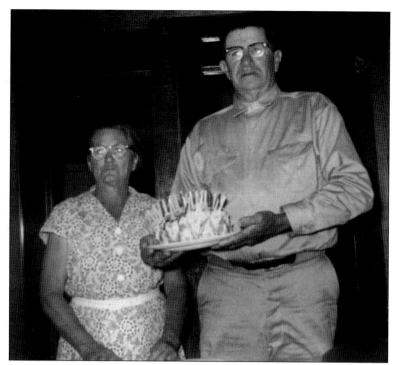

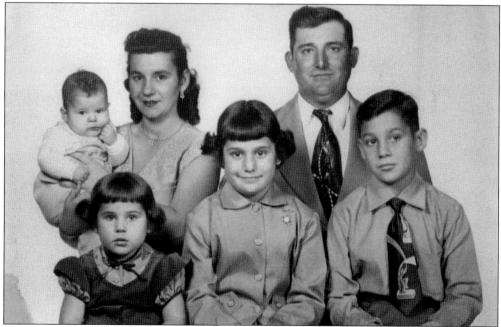

In 1763, the Treaty of Paris gave the lands east of the Mississippi River to England. Many French-speaking people lived there, which meant they would become subjects of Great Britain unless they departed. This led to a migration of these people to French-controlled areas like the Opelousas Territory. Seen here is the Frugé family of Eunice. They are, from left to right, (first row) Glenda Marie Frugé, Drucella Ann Frugé, and Sweenie Joseph Frugé Jr.; (second row) Danny James Frugé, Nellie Grace Johnson Frugé, and Sweenie Joseph Frugé Sr. (Courtesy of the John H. Harper collection.)

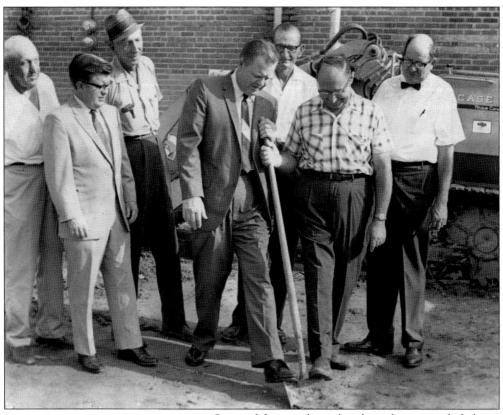

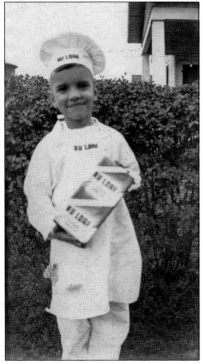

Some of these early settlers from the east included the Fontenots, LaFleurs, Doucets, Frugés, Lagranges, Bonins, and Brignacs. About 50 former Alabama Post settlers established a village along Bayou Courtableau, near present-day Washington. From there, they spread along Bayou Cocodrie and its tributaries. Seen here in 1968 is the groundbreaking ceremony for Elks Lodge No. 1048, on North Union Street in Opelousas. From left to right are L.V. Chachere, Manny Veltin, Errol Amy, exalted ruler Jack Womack (holding shovel), Robert Amy, Jessie Bertrand, and Earl Veillon.

In 1990, attorney Warren A. Perrin filed a petition for an apology on behalf of all Acadians—including Opelousas resident Gerald Mouton, seen here in 1950 in a Nu Loaf chef's costume—from the British Crown for wrongs occurring during the Acadian exile. On December 9, 2003, Queen Elizabeth II's representative, Adrian Clarkson, the governor general of Canada, signed a royal proclamation, now on display at the Acadian Museum in Erath, acknowledging the Crown's role in the deportation and decreeing July 28 an annual Day of Commemoration. (Courtesy of the Louis V. Bernard Jr. collection.)

Three

TOWNS

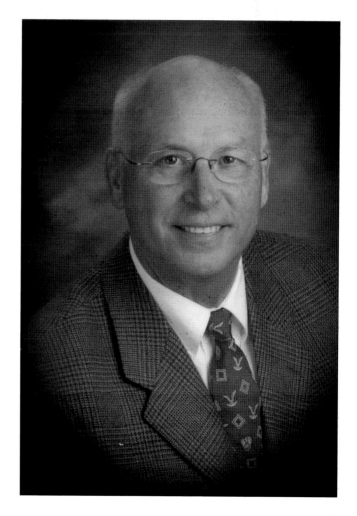

St. Landry Parish began as an expansive territory that was larger than many states and even some countries in Europe. It stretched westward from the steamboat town of Washington across prairies all the way to what was considered Spanish-held Texas. Bayous traversed flat wetlands and were used for transportation. On October 1, 1979, Reggie Dupré of Opelousas, seen here, formed Dupré Transport Inc., which expanded through the years and now has offices in 23 states, Canada, and Mexico.

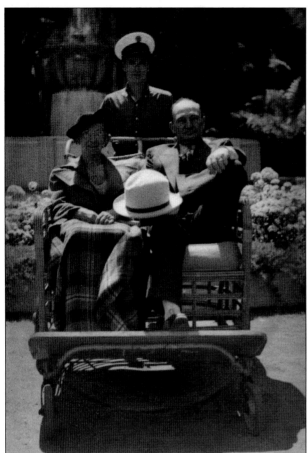

Cankton, in the Coulée Croche section of St. Landry, takes its name from Dr. Louis Aristide Guidry, who was known as "Cank." Legend has it that as a boy he was an avid duck hunter and would signal his family that he was home from a hunt by sounding his duck call: "cank, cank, cank." His family would say, " '*Cank*' *est revenu*," or "Cank" is back, and the nickname stuck. Marie Cecilia Durio Guidry and Louis Aristide "Dr. Cank" Guidry are seen here riding in a rickshaw while visiting Chicago in the 1920s.

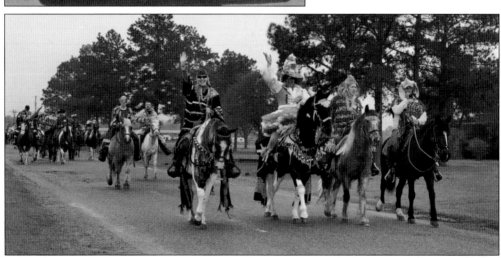

Janet Prudhomme (left) and Amanda Bordelon wave during the 2011 Eunice Courir de Mardi Gras, a traditional Mardi Gras event held in many Cajun communities on the Tuesday before Ash Wednesday. The rural revelry is based on early pagan begging rituals. As Mardi Gras is the celebration of the final day before the austerity of Lent, celebrants overeat and drink and dress in specialized costumes, ostensibly to protect their identities.

St. Landry Parish is situated in the center of Acadiana, a cultural region established by the Louisiana state legislature on June 6, 1971, in recognition of the area's uniqueness and grounded in its "strong French Acadian cultural aspects." Seen here is Dr. Benjamin Guilbeau, an Acadian family doctor who practiced in Grand Coteau, Sunset, and the surrounding communities. Dr. Guilbeau obtained his degree from Western Kentucky University.

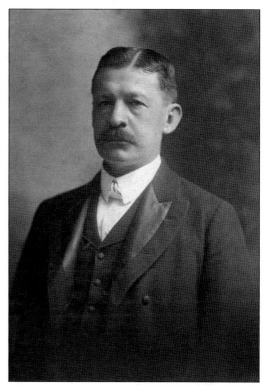

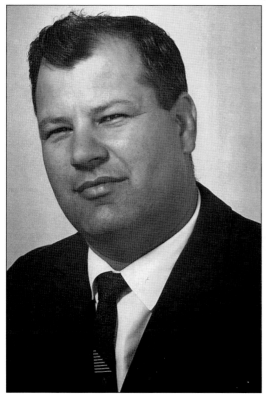

Plaintiff Calvin Roch, seen here, objected to being called a "coonass" by coworkers and filed a lawsuit in order to determine if Cajuns were a legally recognized ethnic group. In 1980, a Louisiana federal district court ruled in Roch's favor by finding that the ethnic slur could not be used to refer to Cajuns, thereby according them protective status under the 1964 Civil Rights Act.

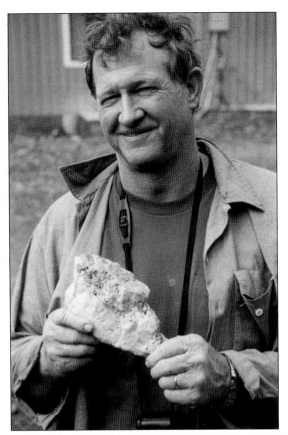

As most counties in the nation inevitably have their roots absorbed into the American mainstream, St. Landry Parish stands almost alone in retaining its unique, complex heritage, one where music, food, spices, culture, and even words are honored by their own festivals. Dan Wiltz, seen here at his gold mine in Alaska, was the owner of Midwest Cooling Tower Services in Krotz Springs. He was an engineer, diver, businessman, pilot, and family man who died tragically in a 2002 plane crash.

In 1782, the Opelousas and Attakapas Districts were inundated by waters from the Atchafalaya River. To protect against such floods, early dwellings and roads were often built on natural levees bordering lower-elevation prairie flood basins. Here, Chook Halphen (left) and Charles Dossman are seen at the Bordelon Motors filling station on December 31, 1933.

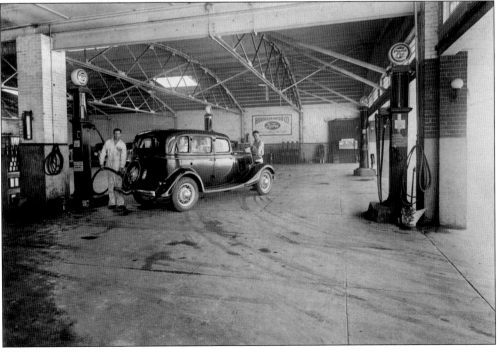

Because of its bountiful natural resources, St. Landry Parish has always been a beacon for immigrants. Since 1957, the Opelousas General Health System has provided care for its citizens. Sidney Sandoz Jr., seen here, served as the board chairman until 1986.

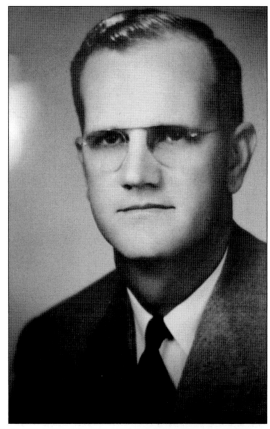

In 1821, Grand Coteau became home to the Academy of the Sacred Heart. Seen here at the University of Louisiana (UL) at Lafayette Alumni House on June 29, 2012, are, from left to right, Warren A. Perrin, the former president of the Council for the Development of French in Louisiana (CODOFIL); Francois Delattre, the French ambassador to the United States; Jacqueline Labat; and attorney John Ashby "T-Jean" Hernandez III, the first chairman of the Francophone Section of the Louisiana State Bar Association and a native of Grand Coteau. T-Jean, who had practiced law with his father, John Ashby Hernandez Jr., died on September 3, 2012. In 2013, Delattre was awarded an honorary doctorate in Francophone studies from UL.

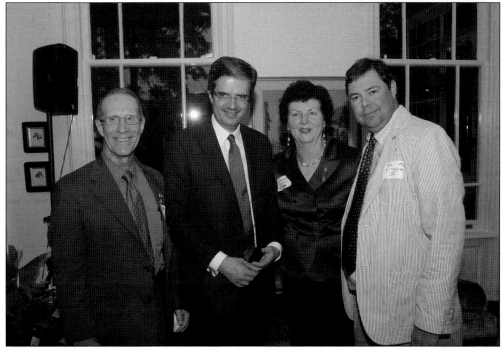

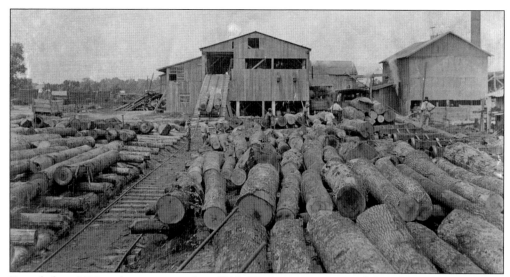

Founded in 1720 and incorporated in 1835, Washington is one of the oldest settlements in Louisiana. Early records indicate that the community was first called Church Landing because the settlement included the first church in the Opelousas District, built in 1774. The area was originally deeded to Jacques Courtableau. The Thistlethwaite Lumber Company, a sawmill located north of Washington, is seen here prior to its 1924 move to Opelousas.

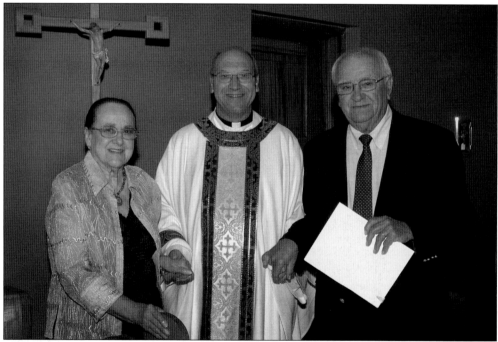

In Leonville, the majority of citizens are Catholics, and they are served by three church parishes: St. Leo the Great, St. Catherine, and St. Jules. During segregation, whites attended St. Leo, blacks went to St. Catherine, and St. Jules served the mulattos. In 2005, the diocese placed one priest in charge and masses were coordinated, resulting in greater integration. Retired judge Joseph A. LaHaye (right) and his wife, Nettie Blanchard LaHaye, were presented with the Bishop's Medal for service to St. Leo by Fr. Ken Domingue. (Courtesy of Nettie Blanchard LaHaye.)

30

Four

CULTURE

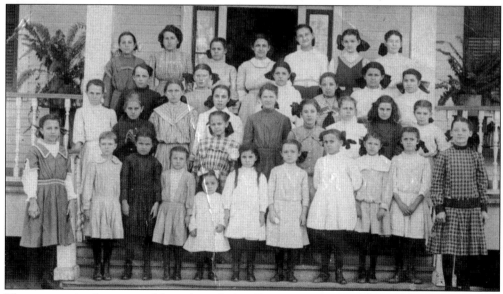

The community that emerged from the turbulent Reconstruction era following the Civil War bore little resemblance to the stratified prewar society. The postwar populace was made up of a small, educated gentry and a large underclass. In 1944, a school for blacks was opened by the Sisters of the Holy Family at Christ the King Mission Chapel in Grand Coteau. Seen here in 1911 are the students at the Little Flower School in Arnaudville. Lucy Maude Morrogh is in the center of the second row wearing a gray dress.

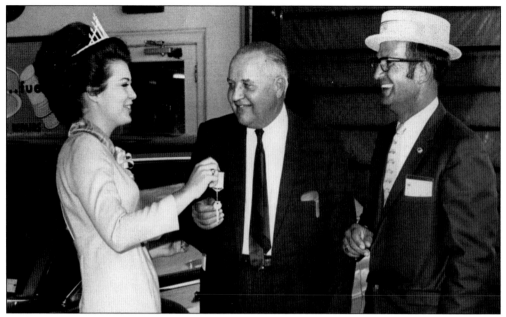

By the early 1900s, many were forced away to seek employment as *engagés*, or indentured workers, until the industrialization of Texas's Golden Triangle—Port Arthur, Orange, and Beaumont—in the 1910s and the development of the oil and gas industry. The availability of the automobile also created a mobile citizenry. Here, Miss Louisiana 1969 Pat Dupre presents the keys to a new car to Archie Quirk Sr. (center) at Bordelon Motors while her father, Gussie Dupre Jr., looks on.

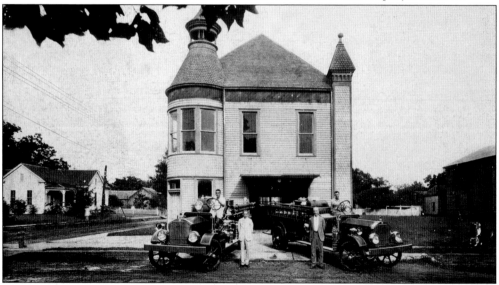

Louisiana's first volunteer fire department was located in Opelousas, which was incorporated by the state legislature in 1853. Seen here in 1924 are members of the Opelousas fire station, known as Hope, Hook and Ladder Company No. 1. They are, from left to right, Jules Trosclair, Didier Lafond, Joe Lafond (chief), and Gus Cahanin. Opelousas is also home to another, more recent first: in the *Times of Acadiana*'s 2002 Best of Acadiana issue, Todd Ortego and Brian "Lil Buck" Burge of the *Swamp 'N' Roll Show* on KDCG-TV were named "The Best Reason to Own a Television Set." (Courtesy of John N. Harper.)

Public education continued the area's cultural evolution in 1916, when compulsory education became the law. In 1921, the Louisiana constitution mandated that only English be spoken in the public schools. Since most students spoke only French, many were humiliated. Seen here in an oak tree at the Sacred Heart Academy in Grand Coteau are the 1963 Sunset High senior class officers. They are, from left to right, (first row) Shirley Miller, president; Lanell Savoie, reporter; Carroll Richard, vice president; (second row) Susan Sibille, secretary; Jimmy Bernard, treasurer; and Lear Olivier, student council representative.

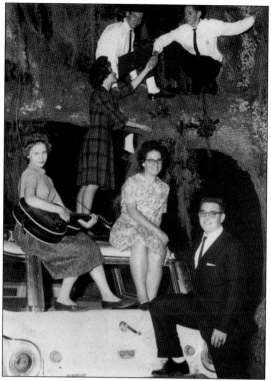

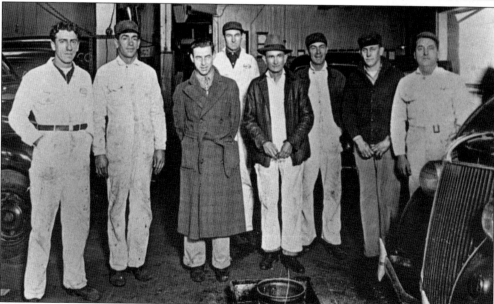

With access to the Mississippi River, the early inhabitants developed a prosperous trading link between what became southwest Louisiana and points along the Mississippi River, especially New Orleans. About a century later, the railroad proved to be a tremendous boost to the region. After the discovery of oil in 1901, the oil industry became a large part of the economy. Seen here in 1930 are Bordelon Motors mechanics, from left to right, R.A. Herpin, Alvin Joseph Fontenot, Marshall Briley, Pat Fontenot, A.C. Culbertson, Louis Taylor, Buster Johnson, and Regis Savoie.

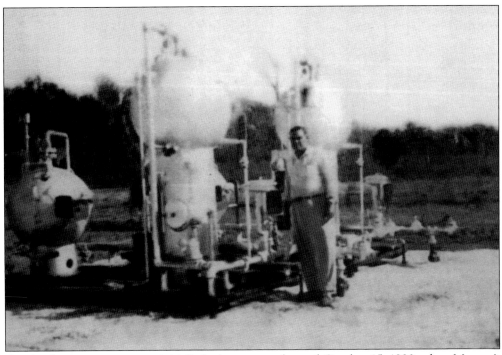

Overland transportation was initially by horse or mule until October 15, 1880, when Morgan's Railroad brought the first passenger train to Opelousas. The railroad caused rapid changes to the Louisiana prairie landscape, bringing an influx of farmers from the Midwest, the beginning of the oil industry, and agricultural mechanization. J.B. Mouton is seen here in 1952 at the North Cankton oil and gas field operated by the Waterbury Company of Opelousas.

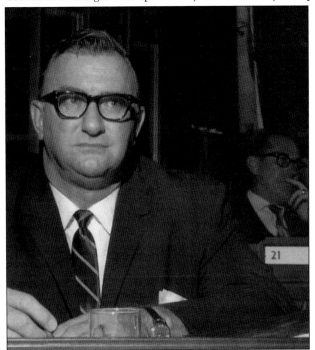

When Opelousas, the state's third-oldest city, founded in 1720, sought regional transportation, the railroad accommodated, connecting St. Landry Parish to the rest of the United States. Opelousas produced many public servants, including Howard Benjamin "H.B." Dejean Jr., a member of the Louisiana House of Representatives from 1968 to 1971, the head of the Louisiana State Democratic Party, and the vice president of the Louisiana Thoroughbred Breeders Association.

Arnaudville is well known for its artists, musicians, and craftspeople, including photographer Peggy Berry, musician Louis Michot; mixed media artist John Daigre; framer Carl Dautreuil, zydeco musician Joe Hall, potter Daryl Harwood, folk artist Lori Henderson, sculptor William Lewis, artist George Marks, fiddle maker Tom Pierce, artist Beth Stark, and potter Linni Tolmachoff. Seen here is Anya Schoenegge Burgess, a luthier (violin maker) and musician.

Prior to the civil rights movement, segregation was the norm in St. Landry Parish. Although blacks contributed significantly to local culture, those who dared to cross racial barriers often faced violent extra-legal retribution. Schools were not integrated until 1969, when Charles Drew High School, an African American school, was merged with Eunice High School. Howard Austin (below), one of the first blacks elected to public office in the 1970s, served for 28 years as a member of the St. Landry Parish Police Jury.

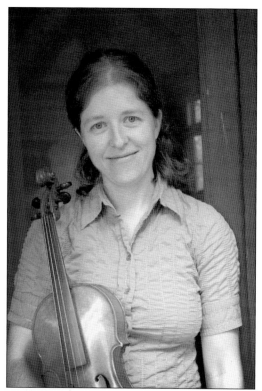

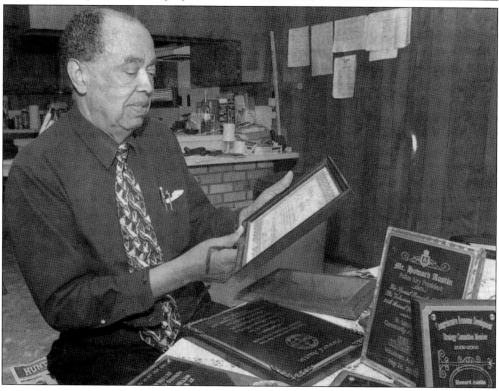

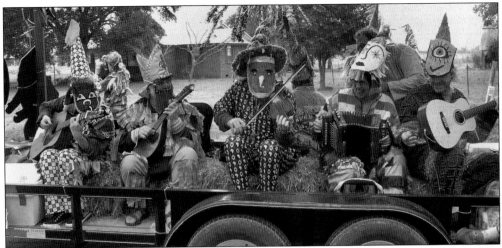

According to professor Dennis L. Bark of Stanford University, locals spoke French from the Civil War up until the mid-1900s. This explains Cajun fiddle player Dennis McGee's admonishment to those who questioned his French ancestry: "McGee, that's a French name. I don't know anyone named McGee who doesn't speak French." This photograph shows musicians in costume on the Faquetique Mardi Gras route, which took the participants to the cemetery where McGee and his wife, Gladys, are buried. There, a priest said a prayer and musicians performed.

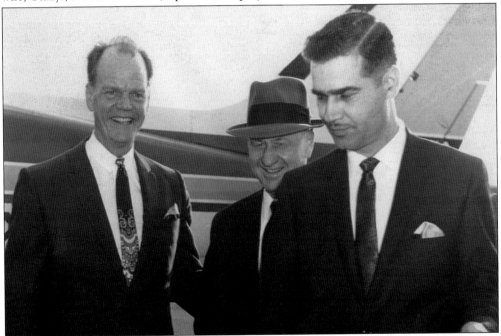

According to professor Bark, "World War II united Americans . . . military forces included about 25,000 Cajuns. They were inclined to view themselves as *les Français*, and others as *les Amériçains*. To survive in the armed forces, the Cajuns were obligated to learn the English language . . . and all of them began to embrace American customs via such equalizing language agents as television, film, and radio." Here, in the 1950s, ABC radio host Paul Harvey (left) is picked up at the Opelousas Airport by W.E. Jones and Johnny Wright (right) of KSLO Radio for a speaking engagement at the Opelousas Junior High School auditorium.

Professor Bark continues: "A milestone in the arbitrary banishment of the language was mandated in 1921 at the constitutional convention which ruled that French would no longer be recognized as an official language. Those who supported the latter approach forgot the value of the French-American affair that had begun 150 years earlier when the Marquis de Lafayette came to the aid of George Washington during America's Revolutionary War." Opelousas airman Remy Bourque is seen here in 1943. He was killed in England during World War II when his B-17 Flying Fortress crashed on January 5, 1944.

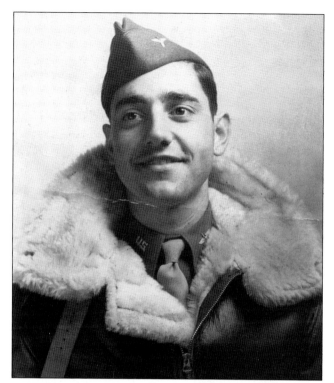

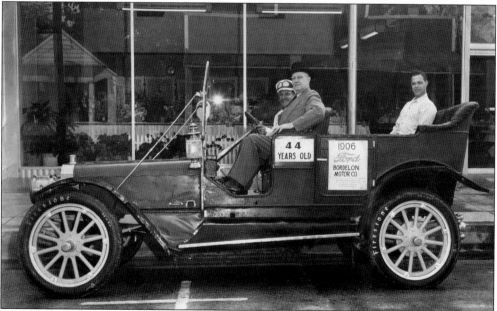

Wells Fargo provided public transportation before the railroad was built. After the railroad came in the late 1800s, people rode the train to get to the parish, as roads were poor. Railroad links opened St. Landry Parish to the rest of the country, increased immigration to the area, and fostered town building. However, nothing was more important than the introduction of the automobile. Seen here in 1950 in a 1906 Ford Model K are, from left to right, Pete Bernard, Martin Bordelon Sr. (driving), and J.Y. Bordelon Sr.

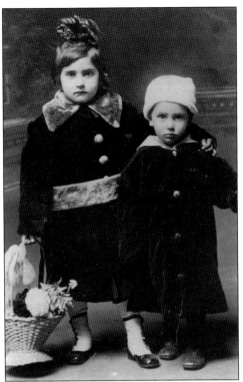

Although the majority of settlers were French, St. Landry was a melting pot of cultures that evolved into a unique citizenry. Seen here in 1916 are Sybil Stafford and Joseph Iseringhausen, whose family had emigrated from Germany in the early 1800s and settled in the Bosco Oil Field area. Stafford graduated from Louisiana State University in education and Iseringhausen was a bus driver, a farmer, and an accountant at the People's Cotton Gin in Cankton.

On June 10, 2012, Vermilionville, the Catalon family, and C.R.E.O.L.E. Inc. honored Goldman Thibodeaux, the vocalist and accordionist for Goldman Thibodeaux and the Lawtell Playboys, with the annual Richard J. Catalon Sr. Creole Heritage Award. In 2013, the award was presented to Willis Prudhomme, who was tutored by famous accordion player Nathan Abshire. Below, on September 5, 2009, from left to right, "Zydeco Joe" Citizen, Thibodeaux, and prodigy Guyland Leday of Frilot Cove perform at the seventh annual Zydeco Breakfast in Opelousas.

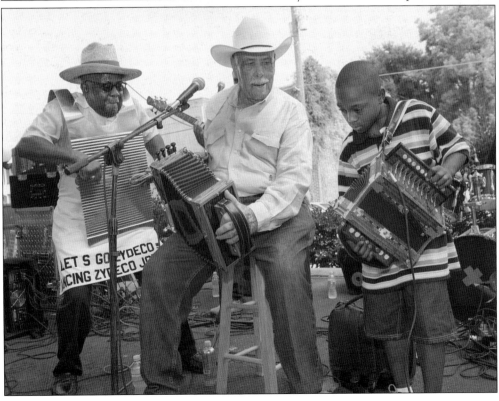

Five

FOLKLIFE

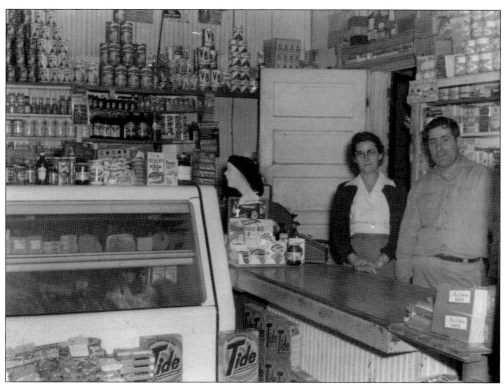

Although it is easier to identify individuals who stand out as remarkable members of the community, the ordinary figures—the postmasters, store clerks, farmers, teachers, and blacksmiths—are no less important. John Marino Jr., the proprietor of Marino's Grocery, an Opelousas landmark for almost 60 years until its closure in 1995, is seen here in November 1956 with his wife, Pearl Brasseaux Marino.

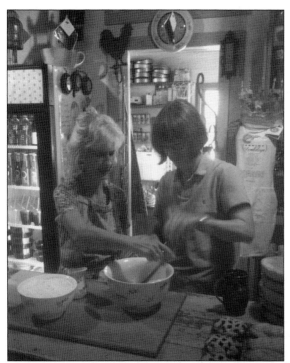

Artists, musicians, and craftspeople of Grand Coteau include photographer Melissa Andries; pastry chef Nancy Brewer, who is seen here on the left making sweet dough tarts with Mary Perrin; musician Henry Hample; chef Jude Tauzin; zydeco musician Jude Taylor; the Chimes Spiritual Musical Group; dancer Yvonne Olivier; artist Jesse Poimboeuf; folk art jeweler Trish Ransom; potter Tanya Schultz; photographer Lucinda Sibille; and photographer John Slaughter, who released the beautiful book *Grand Coteau* in 2012.

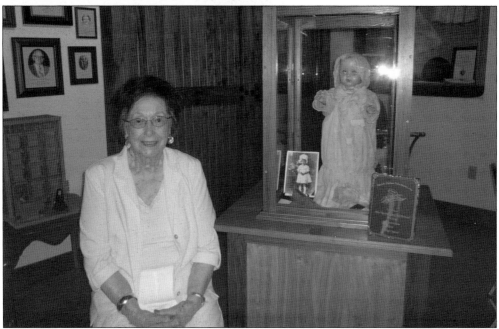

From 1854 to 1929, Orphan Train riders came from the New York Foundling Hospital to Louisiana. The historical event is the subject of the Louisiana Orphan Train Museum in Opelousas, one of the many railway destinations for the thousands of homeless children who were rescued from the streets of New York. Alice Bernard, seen here at the museum, an Orphan Train baby born in New York in 1916, came to Louisiana as a toddler. She spoke English but had to learn the French her new family spoke after her arrival. Today, she is the last Orphan Train survivor in Louisiana.

Some of the artisans of the Sunset area are quilt makers Mary Baum and Christine Hall; fused-glass artists Jerilyn Lavergne and Charla Guidry; potter Annie Hendrix; fiddle maker Marc Taylor; musician Don "Tee Don" Landry; artist, jelly maker, and gourd maker Margaret Brinkhaus; and Curley Taylor, a popular musician seen here performing zydeco in 2010 at the Zydeco Extravaganza, the largest one-day zydeco festival, held annually on Memorial Day.

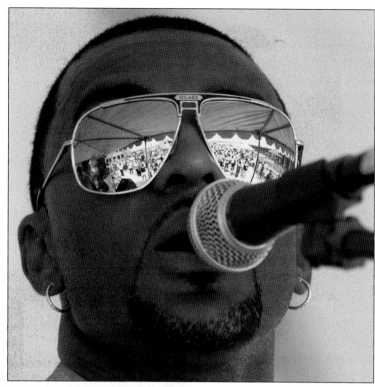

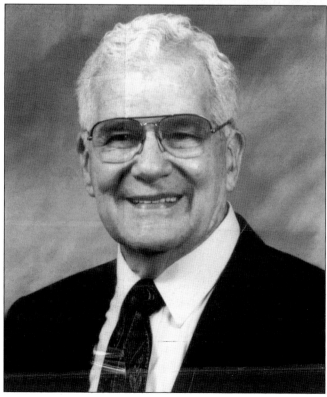

Artists in Opelousas include Creole folklorist, traditional home remedy maker, doll maker, and storyteller Rebecca Henry; card and poster illustrator Julie Martin Greeting; zydeco musician Brad Randall; stained-glass artist Michelle Fontenot; woodworker Frank Dabney; zydeco musician Guyland Ledet; blues musician Roscoe Chenier, who died on February 7, 2013; and James Arthur "J.A." Allen, seen here, who has published *Opelousas Sketchbook* and the *Cajun Coloring Book*.

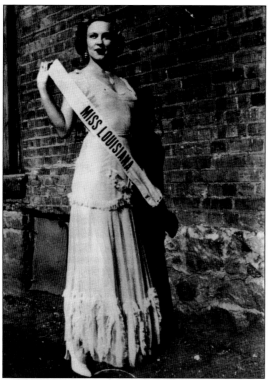

Well-known artisans in Washington include Carolyn Billeaudeau, Millie Boudreaux, Gwendolyn DeJean, Clara Darbonne, Diane Hall, Elijah Harris, June Lowrey, Margaret Mathis, Robert Tinney, and Pat Fontenot. Mildred Kingsbury Nicholson, seen here, who won the first Miss Louisiana contest in 1931, led all Yambilee parades in a silver saddle aboard her prancing horse, wearing a stunning riding habit and holding an American flag. Nicholson, the daughter of a newspaper publisher, was raised in Opelousas and was buried in Washington in 2001.

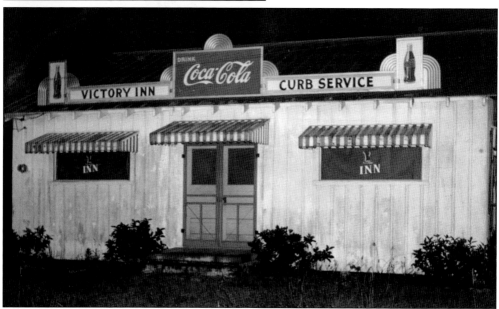

There are two museums in the Krotz Springs area: the Palmetto Municipal Building, located on Highway 10 in Palmetto, which features the permanent exhibit *Palmetto Pictorial History*, and Budden's General Store, located at 165 West Railroad Avenue, which was established in 1934. Johnny Terracina owned the Victory Inn, seen here, during and after World War II. Terracina lived in the back of the restaurant. Located on the old Port Barre road, the name of the restaurant was later changed to The Ranch.

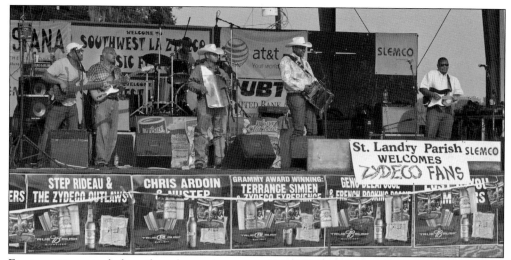

Eunice artisans include quilt maker and crochet worker Bersia Ardoin; musician Morris Ardoin; cowhide chair maker Mary Noonie Bell; Cajun musician Fred Charlie, the bandleader of Acadiana Cajuns; artist Judith Copeland; gardener Elaine Sittig Dupre; violin maker Royne Fontenot; musician Courtney Granger; Cajun accordion player J.C. Labbie, the bandleader of *Ses Amis Cajuns*; crawfish taxidermist Carleen Sittig Landry; Cajun musician Ray Landry, the bandleader of Ray Landry's Cajun Band; violin maker Jessie LeJeune; Cajun Courir de Mardi Gras screen mask makers Georgie and Allen Manuel; cypress swing maker Lawrence Moncla; birdhouse maker Tommy Myers; spinner and weaver Chiquita Morton Reddock; rosary maker Pat Oubre; zydeco musician "Jo Jo" Reed, the leader of the Happy Hill Zydeco Band; soap maker Charles Seale; Cajun musician George Sonnier; Cajun musician Donald Thibodeaux, the bandleader of Cajun Fever; Cajun musician Emile Thibodeaux, the bandleader of the Tasso Loop Ramblers; Cajun fiddler Lindsey Young, a member of the Red Stick Ramblers; and zydeco musician Geno Delafosse, who is seen above with his French Rockin' Boogie Band performing at the Original Southwest Louisiana Zydeco Festival on August 30, 2008, and at right in 2009. On October 10, 2012, Delafosse hosted his 15th annual Fan Appreciation Party.

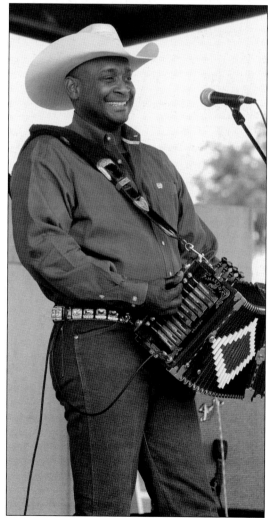

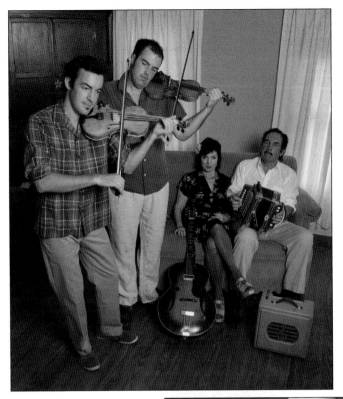

The Savoy Family Cajun Band of Eunice plays traditional yet energetic Cajun music. Marc and Ann Savoy have been performing together since 1977 and have appeared at such prestigious venues as the Newport Folk Festival and the Berlin Jazz Festival, and in the film *Divine Secrets of the Ya-Ya Sisterhood*. Marc also appeared in the film *Southern Comfort*, and Ann has been nominated for three Grammy Awards: for her album with Linda Ronstadt, *Adieu False Heart*; for work with The Magnolia Sisters; and as a producer for the compilation *Evangeline Made: A Tribute to Cajun Music*. Seen here from left to right are Joel, Wilson, Ann, and Marc Savoy. (Courtesy of Gabrielle Savoy.)

Marc Savoy is a recipient of the National Heritage Fellowship Award, while Ann was awarded the Botkin Book Award for *Cajun Music, A Reflection of a People*. Wilson Savoy, as a member of the Grammy-nominated Pine Leaf Boys, appeared on HBO's *Treme* series and won a Grammy in 2013 for *Le Band Courtbouillion*. Joel Savoy was a founding member of the Red Stick Ramblers and cofounded Valcour Records with Lucius Fontenot and Philip LaFargue II, which produced *Le Band Courtbouillion*. Another family member, Gabrielle Savoy, seen here, is an artist and photographer. (Courtesy of Gabrielle Savoy.)

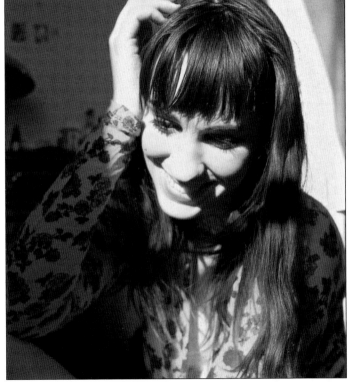

Sarah Savoy is continuing the family musical tradition by performing Cajun music in Paris. Her band gained a reputation in Europe for their driving dance hall Cajun, rousing rockabilly, and sizzling zydeco tunes. Sarah sings in celebration of the modern woman—strong, independent, and fun-loving—rather than only lamenting the traditional position of *la femme abandonnée*, the abandoned woman. Keeping her audiences dancing, Sarah belts out sassy blues and honky-tonk-inspired Cajun songs of the 1940s and 1950s. (Courtesy of Gabrielle Savoy.)

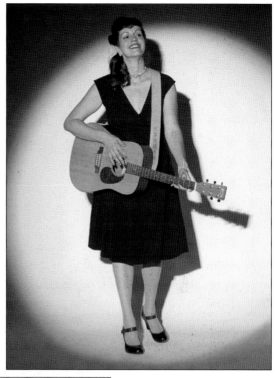

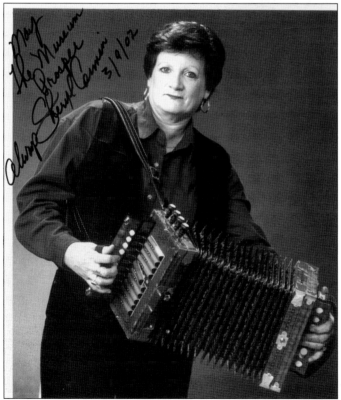

Sheryl Cormier, born in Grand Coteau and raised in Sunset, is one of the first women to break through the traditionally sexist restrictions of Cajun music. Cormier is currently the leader of Cajun Sounds. Learning to play the accordion at age seven, Cormier performed with her parents' group throughout her teens. In 1990, she assembled a group that featured her husband, Russell, on vocals and her son Russell Jr. on drums and recorded *Queen of Cajun Music*, or "La Reine de Musique Cadjine." In 2002, she was named a Living Legend by the Acadian Museum.

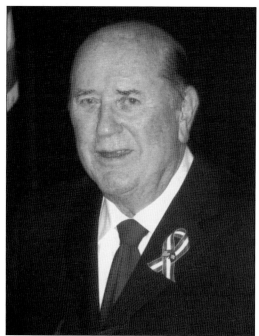

Former Eunice mayor Curtis Joubert, a native of Lawtell, was elected to the US House of Representatives in 1967. He was named a Living Legend by the Acadian Museum in 2006. Joubert was instrumental in creating such Cajun landmarks as the Liberty Theater, the Jean LaFitte National Historic Park and Preserve, the Prairie Acadian Cultural Center, the Cajun French Music Hall of Fame, the Crawfish Étouffeé Cook-Off, and the traditional Eunice Mardi Gras. Joubert was also inducted into the Louisiana State University–Eunice Hall of Fame and the Louisiana Political Hall of Fame.

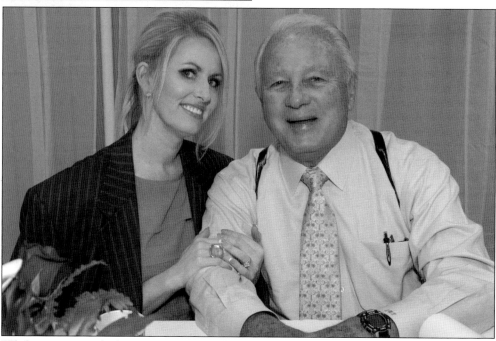

While serving as a freshman congressman for Louisiana's 7th congressional district, Gov. Edwin W. Edwards secured the funding for the Opelousas post office and Lawtell's water district. In 1972, with an unprecedented combination of Cajun and black votes, Edwards was elected to the first of four terms as governor. After serving more than eight years in prison for corruption, Edwards was released on January 13, 2011. *The Governor's Wife*, an A&E reality television series about Edwards and his wife, Trina Scott, debuted in 2013. They are seen here at his induction by the Acadian Museum into the Order of Living Legends on August 4, 2012.

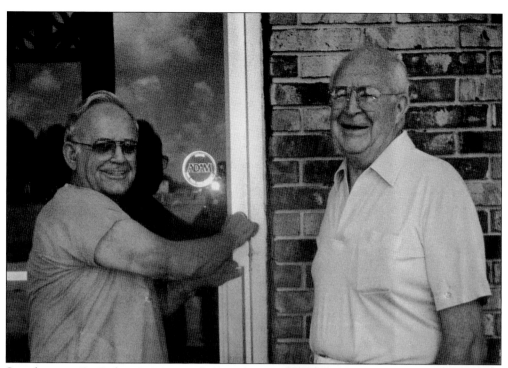

Seen here are Dr. Robert L. Morrow (left) and
Dr. Earl H. Morrogh. Morrow purchased the
St. Francis Clinic in 1948. In 1949, Morrogh
joined him in his medical practice, which served
the people of Arnaudville, Cecilia, Leonville,
Pecaniere, Henderson, Butte La Rose, Port
Barre, and Krotz Springs. They estimated that
each had delivered over 2,000 babies. They
closed their practice in August 1988; however,
they both continued treating the residents of
J. Michael Morrow Memorial Nursing Home.

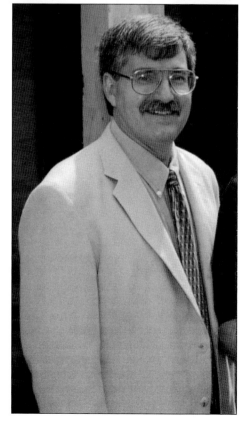

Carl A. Brasseaux, PhD, a retired professor
of history and the director of the Center for
Louisiana Studies, the Center for Cultural
and Eco-Tourism, and the University of
Louisiana at Lafayette Press, is one of the
world's leading authorities on French North
America, with extensive expertise in the
areas of Acadian/Cajun and Creole history
and culture. Brasseaux, a native of Sunset,
holds a doctorate from the *Université de
Paris* and has published 40 volumes on
Louisiana and French North America.

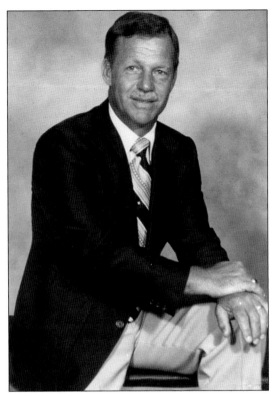

John Bradley (left) was the quintessential educator, devoting his life to helping young people through athletics. Upon his graduation from Southwestern Louisiana Institute (now the University of Louisiana at Lafayette), he returned to his alma mater, Opelousas High School, as a teacher and coach. He served as a principal, supervisor, and assistant superintendent in St. Landry Parish and as the president of the Louisiana High School Athletic Directors' Association. The Opelousas High School football jamboree event is held annually in his honor in the stadium dedicated to his memory. His son John Ed Bradley (below) is a Pulitzer Prize–nominated author of seven novels, many of which draw influence from his hometown of Opelousas and his experience playing football at Louisiana State University in the late 1970s. His writings have been featured in many newspapers and magazines, including the *Washington Post*, *Esquire*, *Sports Illustrated*, and *Louisiana Life*.

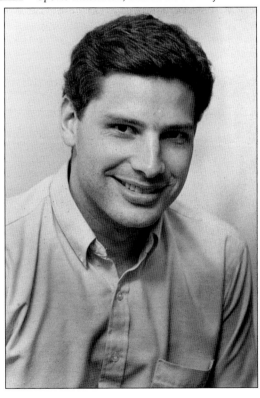

Six

COMMUNITY

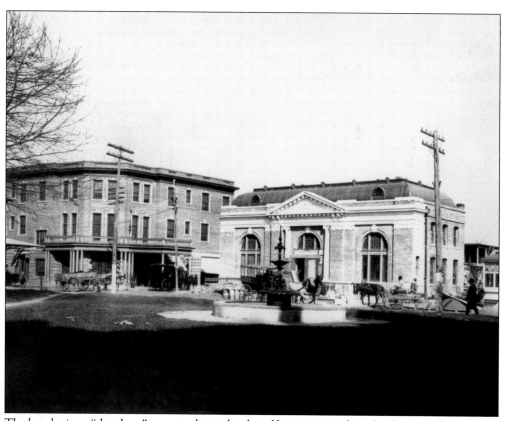

The *boucherie*, or "slaughter," was a tradition developed by necessity where families joined together to provide meat for the week. These gatherings nurtured a sense of community, as did the development of the parish's seat of government in Opelousas. This photograph shows the Lacombe Hotel and Union Bank in 1921, viewed from the corner of Court and Bellevue Streets.

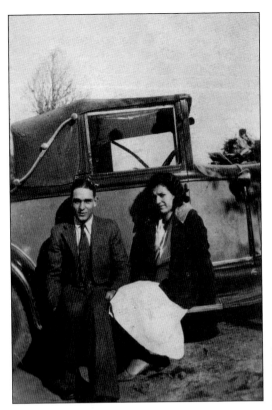

The women's role in shaping the culture of St. Landry cannot be overemphasized. Seen here sitting on the running board of a car are Earl J. Savoie and Wilhelmina Guilbeau, who married on April 21, 1932. Earl, a farmer and school bus driver, served as an alderman for the Town of Cankton from July 1961 to 1965 and then again from July 1969 until his death in 1976. Wilhelmina, a homemaker, was also the first female mayor of Cankton—and the first female mayor in St. Landry Parish. She served from July 1961 to June 1965 and later served as an alderman from July 1976 until June 1981.

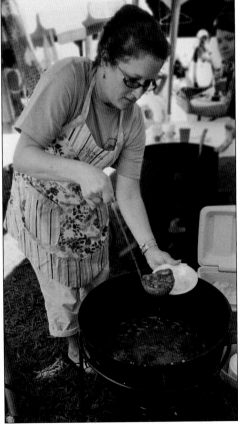

The preparation and enjoyment of food was a relaxing pastime for hardworking citizens. *Roux*, a browned mixture of flour and oil, provided the thick, robust body for gumbo, *sauce-piquante* (a highly seasoned stew), and rice dressing. Spicy condiments, as well as jambalaya, were introduced by the Spaniards. Kelly Pitre of L'Acadie Inn is seen here stirring a pot of crawfish bisque at the World Championship Crawfish Étouffée Cook-Off in Eunice.

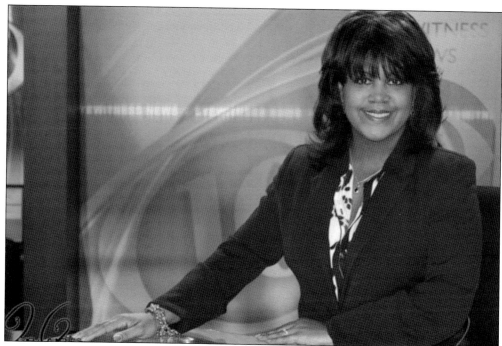

An Opelousas native, Darla Montgomery is one of five children born to Alvarez and Patricia Hertzock. Montgomery co-anchors Eyewitness News for CBS affiliate KLFY-TV10 in Lafayette. She is an Associated Press award–winner for spot news, feature reporting, and public affairs—for a documentary chronicling Fr. Glenn Meaux's mission in Haiti. She was also featured in a Louisiana Public Broadcasting documentary about folk medicine and *traiteurs*. In 1999, one assignment took her to Africa, where she covered St. Martinville's efforts to "twin" with Gorée Island, Senegal.

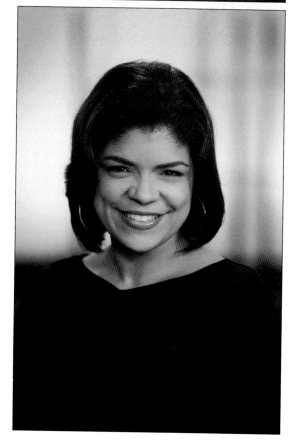

Marcelle Fontenot, a native of Opelousas, earned her mass communications degree with honors at Southern University in 2002. She interned at KATC-TV3 during the summer of 2001 and then joined the news department in August 2004 after producing and hosting *Parental Vision* on KDCG-TV22 in Opelousas for 18 months. She was named the co-anchor of KATC's 6:00 p.m. newscast in June 2006.

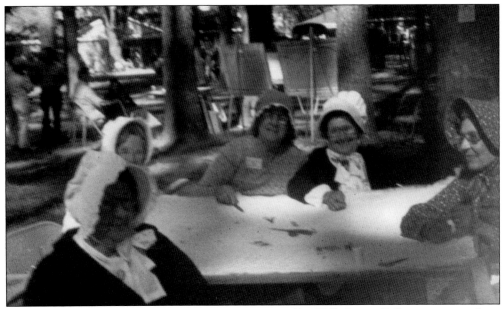

The Cankton Swingers, a senior citizens' group organized by Wilhelmina G. Savoie, are seen here in 1979 wearing their signature bonnets during a quilting demonstration on the grounds of St. Ignatius School and St. Charles Church in Grand Coteau, for the centennial of the church. The members went on trips organized by Iva Clavelle to Canada, staying in the homes of Canadians. From left to right are Eva Savoie, Celeste Mouton, Wilhelmina G. Savoie, Etta Richard, and Mabel Miller.

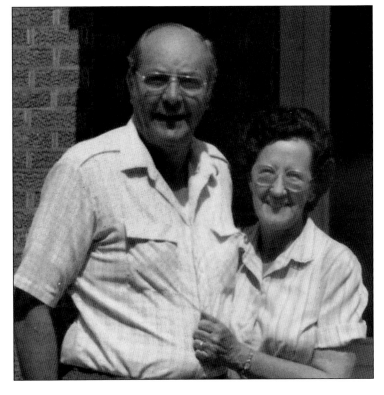

Floyd Andrepont and his wife, Ella Olivier Andrepont, were the owners and operators of Andy's Fried Chicken & Seafood Restaurants and Andrepont Poultry & Supermarket. Both businesses were started at 1145 West Landry Street in Opelousas. Andrepont attended school in Opelousas and graduated from Louisiana State University before teaching agriculture and chemistry for 12 years. He was also a school board member and was active in civic affairs for many years.

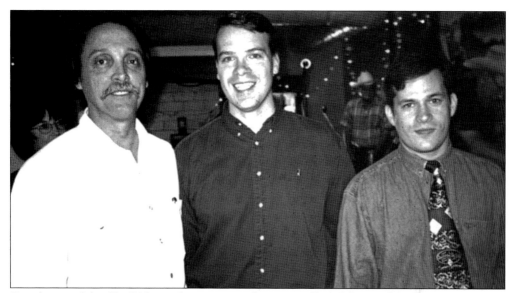

Seen here on May 22, 1999, are three eminent historians (from left to right): Dr. Barry Ancelet, a University of Louisiana at Lafayette professor and the author of *Cajun Country*; Dr. Robert Carriker, the department head of history, geography, and philosophy at the University of Louisiana at Lafayette and the author of *Boudin*; and Dr. Shane K. Bernard, a historian and curator for McIlhenny Company, the son of swamp pop singer Rod Bernard, and the author of *Swamp Pop: Cajun and Creole Rhythm & Blues*; *The Cajuns: Americanization of a People*; and *Cajuns and Their Acadian Ancestors*.

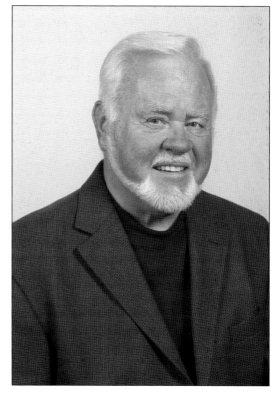

Bobby Dupre, a pillar of the St. Landry Parish community, hosted a radio show on KSLO radio for 35 years. It is now on KDCG/RTN television and on the internet. A prominent and successful Opelousas businessman, Dupre is also a generous philanthropist and supporter of many area charities. The closest to his heart is the Opelousas Area Cerebral Palsy Clinic, where he has served as a board member and organizer of the annual Breakfast with Santa Claus fundraiser, which raises more than $40,000 annually for the clinic.

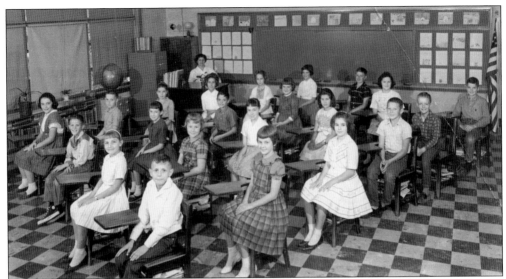

Seen here in 1962 is Lucille Sibille Landry's fourth-grade class at Cankton Elementary. From left to right are (first row) Darylin Savoie, Richard Comeaux, Mary Lynn Menard, and Rickie Meche; (second row) Dennis Savoie, Ruthie Bourque, Sandra Venable, and Debra Bourque; (third row) Diane Meche, Fred Menard, Mona Mouton, and Cynthia LeBlanc; (fourth row) Linda Kilchrist, Brenda Courville, Carmen Hebert, and Frederick Babineaux; (fifth row) Linda ?, Cleo Iseringhausen, and Harry Lee Meyers; (sixth row) Shirley Meyers, Kenneth Comeau, and Russell ?.

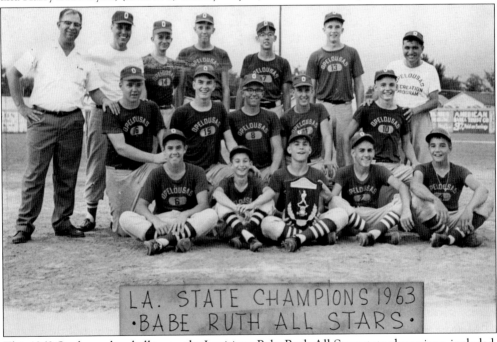

This 1963 Opelousas baseball team, the Louisiana Babe Ruth All-Stars state champions, included, from left to right, (first row) Chris Dunbar, Randy McDaniel, Jay Stelly, Raymond Stelly, and Frank "Chip" McCardell; (second row) Jay Cormier, Vaughn Walton, Neil Soileau, Albert Going, and John Daigle; (third row) George O'Neal, Tommy Murrell, Peter Workman, Gene Mauch, Charles Soileau, Sherman Edwards, and Wray Guilbeau.

Seven

ENTERTAINMENT

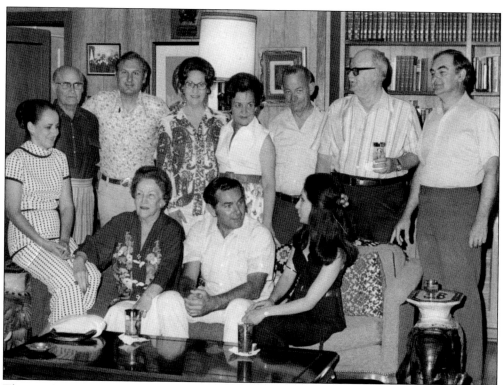

The Opelousas district attorney's office hosted Aaron Stovitz, the prosecutor of the Charles Manson murder trial in Los Angeles, in November 1972 for the St. Landry Bar Association's annual meeting. Seen here at the home of Assistant District Attorney Morgan Goudeau III are, from left to right, (first row) Nettie Blanchard Lahaye, Lessley Gardiner, Stovitz, and Alma Goudeau; (second row) District Attorney "J.Y." Fontenot, Morgan Goudeau III, Lucille Fontenot, Mickey Pavy, Judge Garland Pavy, Judge Lessley Gardiner, and Judge Joseph A. Lahaye.

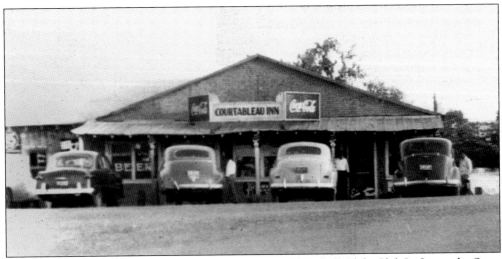

Dance clubs like the Southern Club, Tee Maurice, the Chinaball Club, Club La Lune, the Step-In-Club, the Green Lantern, the Silver Slipper, and the Happy Landing were popular. However, during Lent, Catholics refrained from such dances. In 1950, the Courtableu Inn, a successful dance club located in Port Barre on Bayou Teche, was owned by Oscar Bordelon, the grandfather of swamp pop legend Rod Bernard. (Courtesy of the Johnnie Allan Collection.)

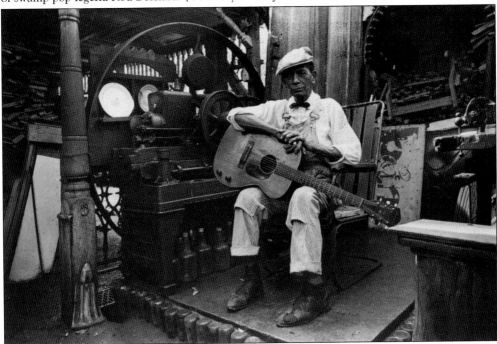

Families often invited their *voisins* (neighbors) to a *veillée* (social gathering) where music was enjoyed. Guests were served *tarts à la bouillie* (sweet dough pies) and home-brewed beer. *Bourré*, a card game, was played by the men in a *cabine*, or outbuilding. According to professor Dennis L. Bark of Stanford University, "The earliest instrument used to make Cajun music was the fiddle. As in the past, it is often played today with the accompaniment of a guitar and an accordion." Seen here is Rosenberg "Buck" Hebert, an Opelousas furniture refinisher known for his storytelling prowess and his museum. (Courtesy of John Slaughter.)

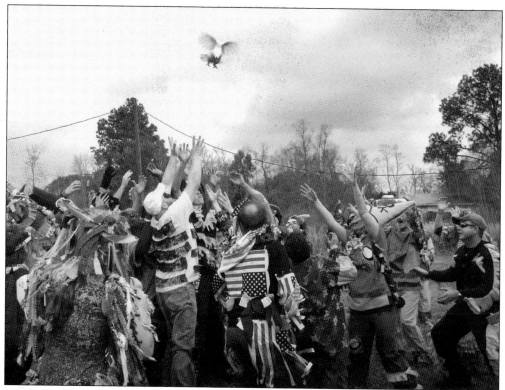

Mardi Gras brought communities together. Revelers are seen here trying to catch the chicken as part of the festivities at Eunice's Faquetique Mardi Gras, founded in 2006 by members of the Red Stick Ramblers and other area musicians as a more traditional alternative to the main Eunice Courier de Mardi Gras. No beads are allowed at the event and all music must be played on instruments.

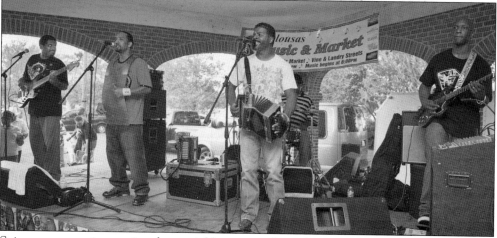

Soirees were evening parties where neighbors enjoyed a night of *rondes de danses*, with five types of music in a designated order. The guitar was introduced to local music around 1800 by the Spanish. Stephen Joseph "Step" Rideau and the Zydeco Outlaws are seen here at the Opelousas Music and Market on May 23, 2008. Rideau was born in 1966 in Lebeau but did not play music until he moved to Houston in the mid-1980s.

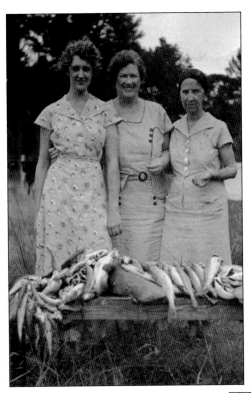

The Catholic Church required its members to abstain from eating meat on Fridays, with the idea that people would limit their food to vegetables and grains. However, meat was considered to be the flesh of warm-blooded land animals, whereas fish are cold-blooded creatures. Using this technicality, people began consuming fish on days of abstinence. Thus, seafood became a staple on Fridays, adding to other culinary delicacies. This early 1930s photograph shows, from left to right, Hortense Guidroz, Lucy Maude Morrogh Guidry, and Cecile Durio Guidry as they prepare to cook fish.

According to his 2010 biography, *But He Dies Not*, by Peter and Suzanne Guerra, Fr. J. Verbis Lafleur was an exceptional man. On April 2, 1938, he celebrated his first mass in St. Landry Catholic Church. He joined the Army Air Corps in 1941. On September 7, 1944, Fr. Lafleur gave his life while aboard a torpedoed "hell ship" carrying American prisoners of war. On December 7, 2005, the dedication of the Fr. Lafleur Shrine in St. Landry Catholic Church was held, and the Fr. Lafleur Monument was dedicated on September 7, 2007.

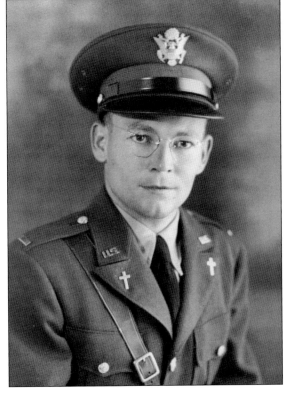

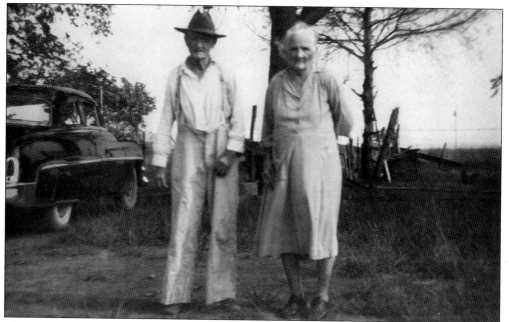

The Great Depression changed the lives of farmers. Many lost their land, while those who did not went into subsistence farming, growing what was needed to survive, such as cotton, sweet potatoes, corn, and okra. Most had a small pasture, a large vegetable garden, a pig, and a milk cow. Farmers Ozema and Genevieve Bertrand are seen here in the 1930s.

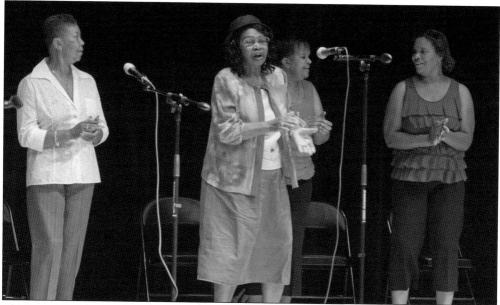

The roots of zydeco are found in *juré*, a form of hand-clapping and foot-stomping used by black field hands to pray and give thanks. This music was called LaLa or *la musique Creole* and was popular at rural house parties in southwest prairie towns. It is best represented by the recordings of Creole accordionist Amédé Ardoin. Seen here on June 5, 2010, at the Delta Grand Theatre is a *juré* demonstration led by Cecilia Broussard (center) with, from left to right, Mary Bias, Vergie Mayon, and Leatha Bergeron.

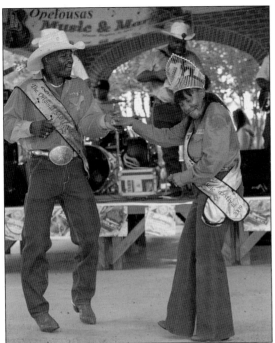

When soldiers returned from World War II, Cajun and Creole music, a combination of old French songs, swamp pop, and blues, emerged as a symbol of ethnic pride. Here, on May 28, 2010, Jake and Sandra Davis dance to the music of Poncho Chavis and the Magic Sounds at the Opelousas Music and Market concert. The Davises were crowned the 2009–2010 king and queen of the 28th annual Original Southwestern Zydeco Festival in Plaisance.

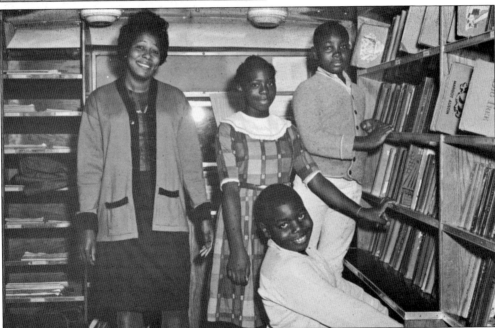

Herman Fuselier, the food and culture editor at the *Daily Advertiser* and the *Times of Acadiana* and the host of *Zydeco Stomp* on KRVS radio, has written, "Cajun music is the waltzes and two-steps played by the white descendants of the Acadians. Zydeco is the R&B-based accordion grooves of black Creoles. Creole has 100 different definitions. But, when it comes to zydeco, it refers to the descendants of slaves, free people-of-color, and mixed-race people of this region." Black children are seen here in a bookmobile in the 1950s. (Reprinted from the *Saline Gazette*; courtesy of Avery Island Inc. archives.)

Fuselier agrees with the definition of zydeco provided by the *Daily Post* newspaper of North Wales in the United Kingdom: "Zydeco is the black dance music of southwest Louisiana which fuses old Creole tunes and rhythms with blues and soul and more recently funk and hip-hop to create an infectious dance groove." Leon Chavis, the son of Joseph "Chopper" Chevis, is seen here performing at the Zydeco Extravaganza, an event founded in 1986 by the Cravins family as an extension of a radio program hosted by Donald and Charles Cravins.

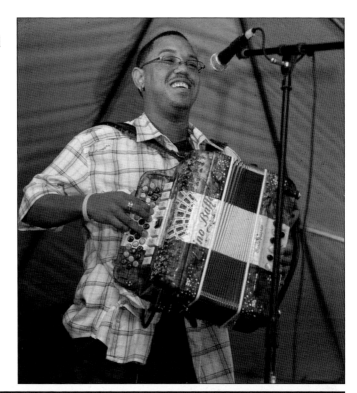

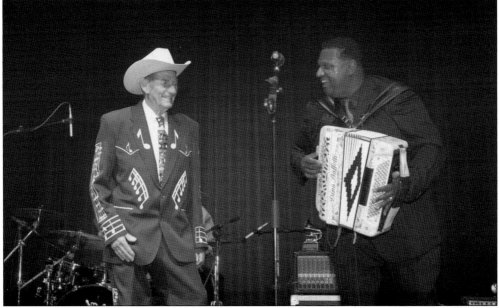

"Chubby" Carrier (right) and the Bayou Swamp Band have been busy touring the country since winning the Grammy Award in the Zydeco/Cajun category on February 14, 2011, for their album *Zydeco Junkie*. Carrier and his band have been featured in local and national print, radio, and television stories. An editorial in the *Opelousas Daily World* with the headline "Tell the world 'Chubby' Carrier is here" concluded by saying, "We can all take pride in it." Carrier is seen here with legend D.L. Menard performing at the Louisiana party at the 2011 Grammys.

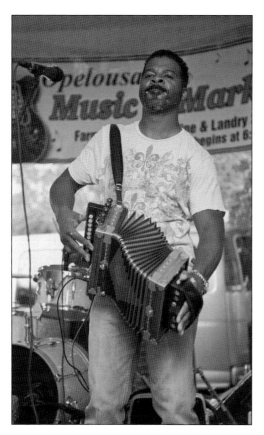

According to the 1995 article "Houston Zydeco as a Mediated Tradition" by John Minton of the Indiana University Folklore Institute, "Notwithstanding its roots in older rural traditions, the genre as currently recognized represents a relatively recent folk/popular syncretism forged in urban, semi-professional performance venues such as the neighborhood taverns and Catholic halls of Houston's Frenchtown district, an enclave attesting to the ongoing rural-to-urban migration of 20th century Creoles." "Step" Rideau, seen here, who is currently based in Houston, has established himself as one of the most prolific zydeco performers.

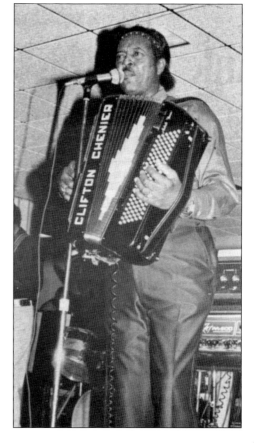

St. Landry Parish is the cradle of zydeco. It is the birthplace of Grammy winners Clifton Chenier, seen here, as well as Rockin' Sidney (Sidney Simien), Queen Ida (Ida Lewis), and Terrance Simien. A more recent zydeco original in the parish was the three-day grand opening, on May 9, 2012, of Miller's Zydeco Hall of Fame in Lawtell. Built in 1947 as Richard's Club, the place has launched the careers of dozens of zydeco musicians. B.B. King, John Lee Hooker, and other blues stars have played there as well. New owners Dustin and Nichole Miller have revived the classic roadhouse.

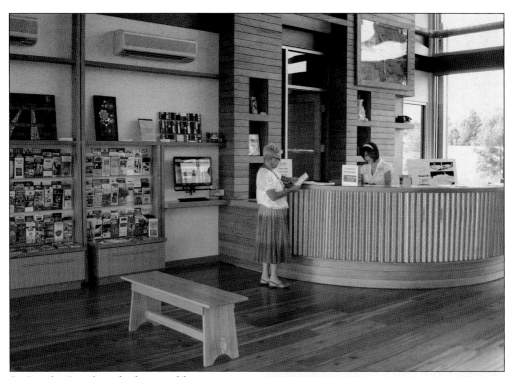

St. Landry Parish is the home of famous athletes, musicians, chefs, and artists, but now it has a new claim to fame: the only "green" visitor center in Louisiana and one of the few in the United States. Celeste D. Gomez, the director of the St. Landry Tourist Commission, says, "As soon as the signage was placed along interstate highway I-49, tourists began stopping at our new Visitor Center." Seen here are Claire White (left) and Stephanie Kramer, travel counselors at the center.

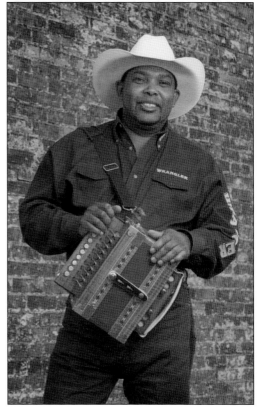

According to Opelousas mayor Don Cravins Sr., "Jeffery Broussard has long been respected as one of the greatest accordion players to ever grace our beautiful Creole culture." From his humble beginnings, Broussard, seen here, a native of Frilot Cove, has become an ambassador of Creole heritage. He began his career with traditional Creole zydeco, playing drums in his father's band, Delton Broussard and the Lawtell Playboys, then moved on to develop the nouveau zydeco sound with Zydeco Force. He eventually returned to traditional zydeco with Jeffery Broussard and the Creole Cowboys. (Courtesy of Philip Gould.)

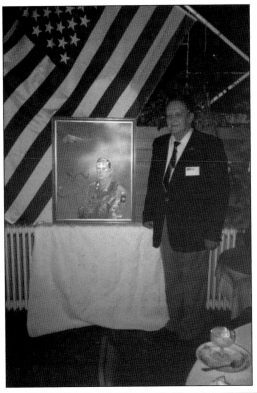

Pathfinders were volunteer paratroopers specially trained to jump into enemy territory to mark landing and drop zones. Lawtell native Lt. Col. G. Wilfred Jaubert, the first American to land in the drop zones of Holland during World War II, is seen here on September 17, 1984, next to a painting by his son Jack Jaubert depicting a historic Pathfinder jump that was part of the largest airborne operation in history. The painting was donated to the National Liberation Museum in Nijmegin, Netherlands. Jaubert, who died in 1987, piloted Gen. Dwight D. Eisenhower during World War II.

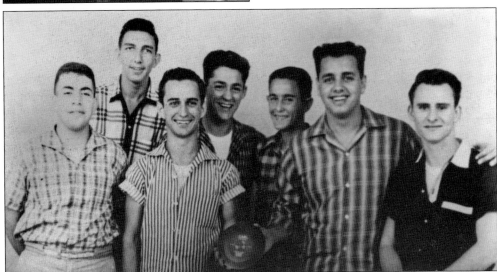

Rod Bernard, born in 1940 in Opelousas, helped to pioneer the musical genre known as swamp pop, which combined New Orleans–style rhythm and blues, country and western, Cajun, and Creole music. As a child, he absorbed the traditional French music performed in his grandfather's dance hall, the Courtableu Inn, in Port Barre, where he heard the music of Aldus Roger, Jimmy C. Newman, and Clifton Chenier. Seen here in 1958 are the members of his band, all fellow Opelousas Senior High School students (from left to right) J.V. Terracina, Marion Presle, Bernard, Charles Boudreaux, Oscar Bernard, Mike Genovesé, and Willie Harmon. (Courtesy of the Shane K. Bernard collection.)

Jim Olivier, a retired broadcaster, singer, and businessman, died on April 13, 2008. A Sunset native, Olivier hosted *Passe Partout*, an early-morning bilingual news program, for 25 years. He also hosted *Meet Your Neighbor* on KLFY-TV, promoted local music, and reported news in French. In 1980, Olivier began a music recording career, releasing the hit "Brasse le Couche Couche." In addition, Olivier researched the Kennedy assassination for more than 30 years and became an authority on the subject. Leaving broadcasting in 1995, he partnered with his wife, Anna, to start Jim Olivier's Home Improvement Company.

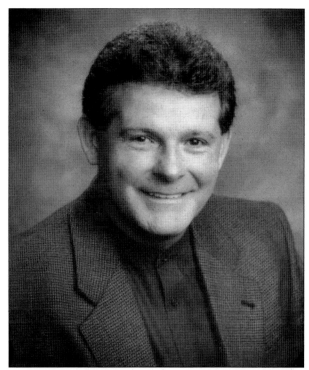

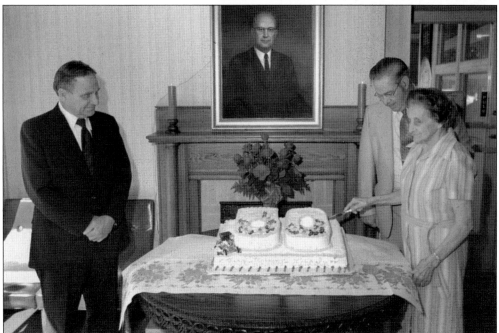

Founded by Martin Bordelon Sr., Bordelon Motors has served motorists throughout the greater Opelousas area since 1916. After being affiliated with the company since 1962, Richard Bordelon, the grandson of the founder, purchased the company on December 29, 1987. Seen here in 1976 at the Bordelon Motors 60th anniversary celebration are, from left to right, Warren Bordelon, J.Y. Bordelon, and Felicity Andrepont Bordelon.

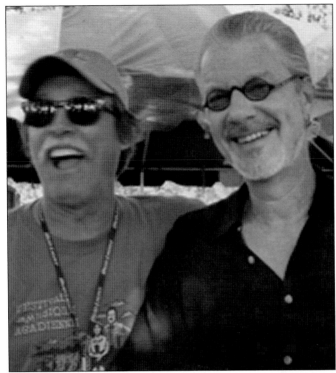

According to professor Dennis L. Bark, "Cajun and Creole music made its debut as a unifying element of the cultures that non-Francophones could enjoy. It became increasingly so as a result of the first Tribute to Cajun Music held in Lafayette in 1974, thanks in large part to Dewey Balfa, who argued that the music was an 'under-appreciated cultural treasure.' " That event was arranged by the Council for the Development of French in Louisiana (CODOFIL) and there was doubt about how successful it would be. Organizer Dr. Barry Ancelet, seen here on the left with musician Sam Broussard in 2010, wondered what would happen if no one attended.

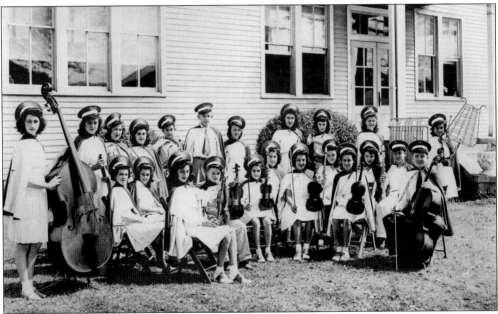

Dr. Ancelet had good reason to worry because, in 1965, Burton Grindstaff, a journalist for the *Opelousas Daily World*, had written a highly condescending article that was critical of the music and verged on the insulting. In the end, it was attended by 12,000 people in a coliseum with a seating capacity of 8,000. Presented entirely in French, the concert was a smashing success that resulted in an annual event called Festivals Acadiens et Creoles. The Academy of Immaculate Conception (now Opelousas Catholic) orchestra is seen here in 1941.

On October 15, 2012, Lafayette government officials gathered at the Chenier Center, named after Clifton Chenier, to accept this photograph of the "King of Zydeco." The famous musician won a Grammy for his 1983 album *I'm Here* and traveled the world until his death in 1987. The photograph of Chenier was taken by Philip Gould at the March 26, 1974, Tribute to Cajun Music. James H. Domengeaux, the nephew of CODOFIL founder and Rep. James Domengeaux, purchased the photograph in 2012 and donated it to the Chenier Center. (Courtesy of James H. Domengeaux.)

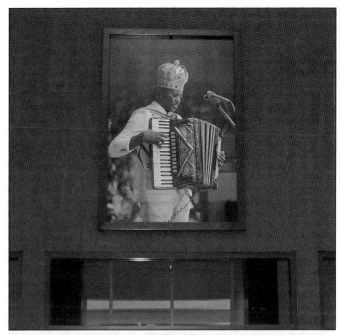

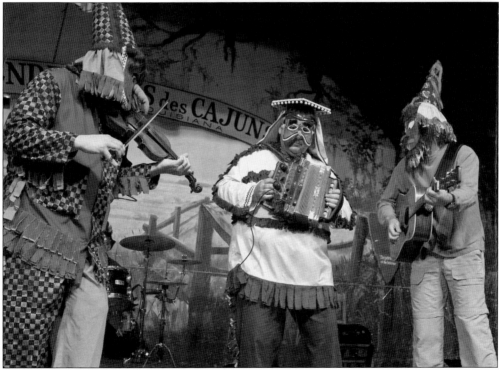

Because of its great diversity, St. Landry Parish is one of the most distinctive of all the Acadiana parishes. In Eunice, the Liberty Theater presents a weekly *Rendezvous des Cajuns* radio show. Hosted by Dr. Barry Ancelet, it features local artists playing traditional French music. Seen here is the Liberty Theater Mardi Gras show on February 21, 2009. Performing on stage are, from left to right, Terry Huval, Reggie Matte, and Bobby Dumatrait of the Jambalaya Cajun Band.

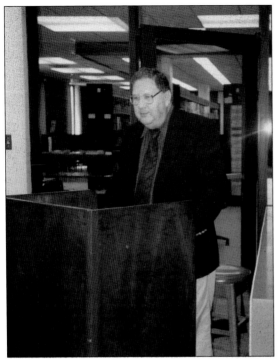

Dr. Claude F. Oubre, a professor of history at Louisiana State University–Eunice (LSUE), died on January 13, 2011. A noted scholar of Louisiana history and folklore, Oubre authored or coauthored several books, including *Forty Acres and a Mule: The Freedman's Bureau and Black Land Ownership*, *Creoles of Color in Bayou Country*, and *The King's Road*. Oubre served as the St. Landry Parish superintendent of schools from 1988 to 1990 before returning to teach at LSUE.

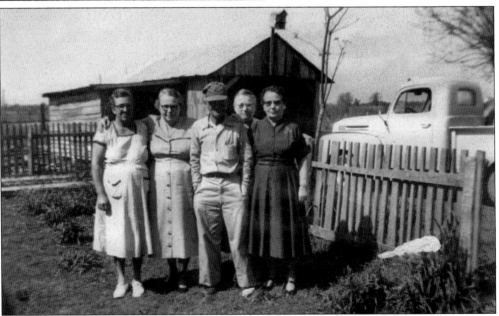

According to professor Dennis L. Bark, "Daily exposure to English, coupled with continuous punishment for speaking French in the classroom or on the playground, did not Americanize Cajun school children immediately, but the national crisis of World War II made the use of English *de rigeur*, thus many Cajun parents declined to teach their French dialect to their children, viewing it as a shameful impediment to social and economic advancement. Punishment took varied forms and was highly effective." Seen here in 1955 are, from left to right, Agnes Brown, Ezar Dupré, Leonard Dupré, Mamie Pitre, and Anna Belle Brown.

In 2005, Casa Azul Gifts was opened in Grand Coteau by Patrice Melnick, seen here, and Randi Kaufman, both New Orleans residents. Melnick was a 2013 recipient of the Public Humanities Programming Award from the Louisiana Endowment of the Humanities, after writing the autobiographical book of hope *Po-boy Contraband*. In 2006, she started open-mic nights that included authors. Established in 2010, the Festival of Words Cultural Arts Collective showcases the literary arts with a festival in November. The venue has since moved to the Thensted Center in Grand Coteau.

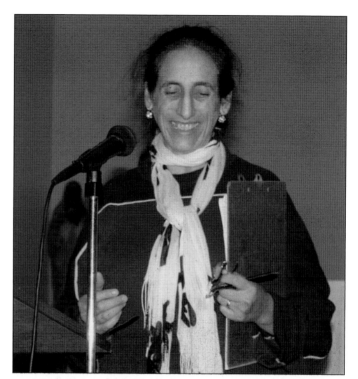

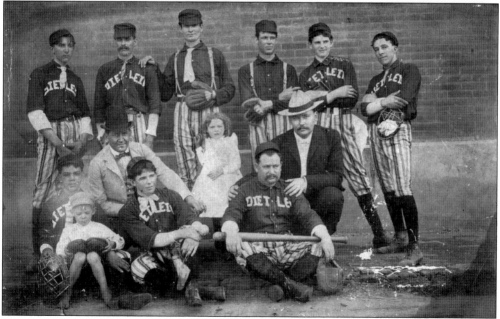

The 1895 Jacobs Dietlein and Wholesale Grocery baseball team, included, from left to right, (first row) ? Dietlein, F. Cliff Allen, and Octave Durio; (second row) Charlie Heno, Fritz Dietlein, Mary Hollier (mascot), and Isidore Isaac; (third row) Willie Eckert, A. Halphen, "Hop" Hillier, ? Hollier, J. Arthur Allen, and Clarence Reynolds. More recently, the Louisiana State University–Eunice baseball team has won the National Junior College Athletic Association Division II World Series an amazing four times in the last eight years.

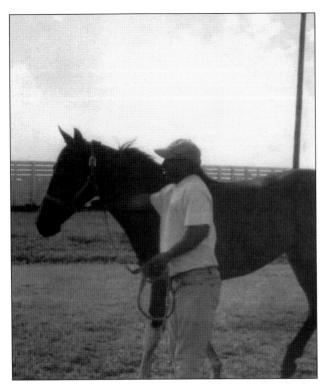

On July 21, 2012, tribal members of the Attakapas tribes of Louisiana gathered to celebrate their reemergence as a people. For decades, the Attakapas were said to have been extinct. However, "they had only gone underground," according to Martha LeJeune, a member of the Eagle Band of the Attakapas. "The original name of the tribe had been Ishak," said Carroll "K.K." Taylor of the Opelousas band, who is seen here walking his horse. On May 1, 2012, the Louisiana Attakapas Opelousas Prairie Tribe Inc. obtained corporate status.

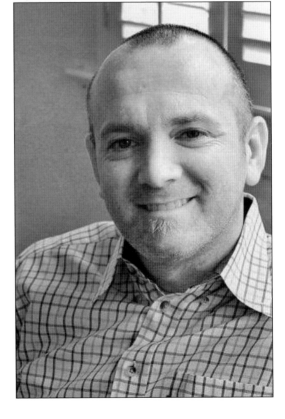

Well-known blues musician Gitlo performed at NUNU Arts and Culture Collective in Arnaudville in August 2012. His performance was part of the center's Artists As One Voice Last Sunday Showcase. NUNU, a center of cultural reemergence for St. Landry Parish, is located at 1510 Bayou Courtableau Highway. Seen here is cofounder George Marks, a visual artist and visionary for cultural tourism.

Hunting has always been popular in the area, and most rural families had dogs to flush game during the hunt. Because rabbits reproduce rapidly, there was always an abundant supply. In the second half of the 1800s, many families depended upon wild game for food. The Bernard family, from the Opelousas area, is seen here in 1880. (Courtesy of the Louis V. Bernard Jr. collection.)

As was common in the early 1900s, many students had to miss school to work on the farm milking cows and picking *ramassant* (figs) and *coton* (cotton). Children learned early that every hand was vitally important for the family's collective well-being. Seen here are, from left to right, Martin Roy Sr., Mildred Sandoz Briggs, and Sidney Sandoz Jr., as Uncle Sam, posing with a new 1941 Oldsmobile before the 1941 Fourth of July parade.

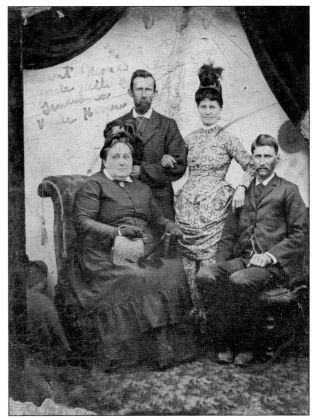

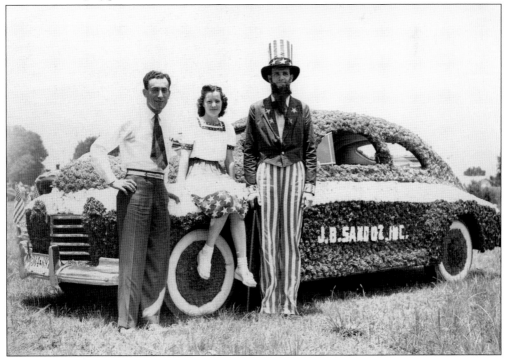

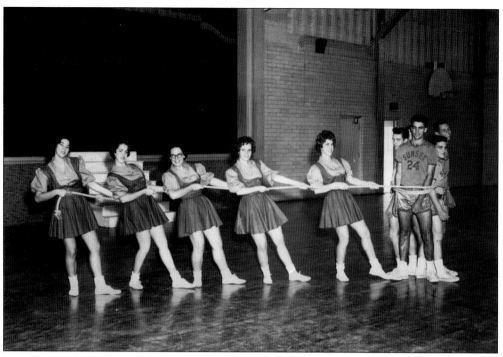

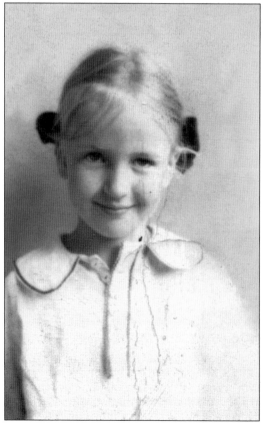

Early schools had no lunchrooms. Children came to school with their own lunch pails, commonly filled with leftover rice and gravy, meat, and bread. Seen in the fun 1962–1963 Sunset High School photograph here are, from left to right, cheerleaders Dale Bonvillain, Patty Dejean, Lanell Savoie, Susan Sibille, and Vickie Dejean and basketball players Elmer Savoie, Victor Lavergne, Bobby Fox, and Lear Olivier.

The Lastrapes family is original to the Opelousas District, beginning with Jean-Henri Lastrapes de Peyrens, who was born to Barthélémy Lastrapes and Laurence Varnéde on October 18, 1753, in Bordeaux, France. He emigrated from France to Spanish Louisiana. On October 14, 1790, he married Céleste Geneviève Boisdoré. Seen here is Alice Lastrapes Carlin, who, after graduating from Opelousas High School in 1948, worked for abstractor Roy Edwards and then clerk of the court Harold Sylvester.

Eight

TRADITIONS

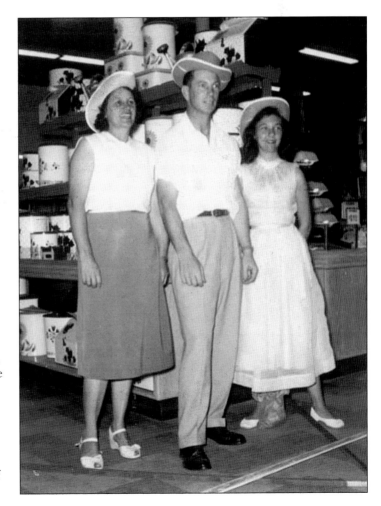

While many pioneer settlers gave up the practice of making *la cotonnade* (homespun cloth) after a few generations in the area, some artisans maintained their production. They eventually became renowned for "Acadian homespun," which came to the attention of national collectors. The craft died out when cloth was made available in local stores such as J.W. Lows. Seen here in that store in the 1950s are, from left to right, Maude Guidry, Leon Huckabee, and Dorothy Babineaux. (Courtesy of Joyce Bodin Lagrange.)

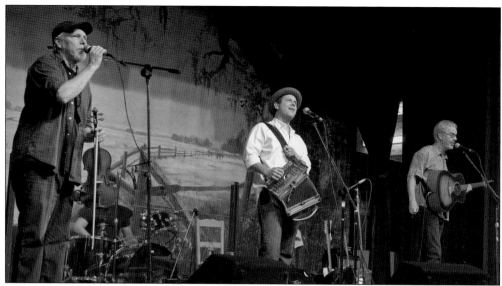

According to professor Dennis L. Bark, "The introductory leaflet that accompanies a CD recording of the Savoy-Doucet Cajun Band provides a marvelous description of a country evening: 'A small bonfire crackles . . . on one side of the yard, husky men wearing big gloves and tall rubber boots tend the steaming crawfish pots. On the other side, musicians sit on wooden benches, bowing, strumming, striking, and squeezing a swirling kaleidoscope of sounds.' " Seen here on October 18, 2008, are, from left to right, David Greely, Steve Riley, and Sam Broussard of the Mamou Playboys, playing at their 20th anniversary performance at the Liberty Theater.

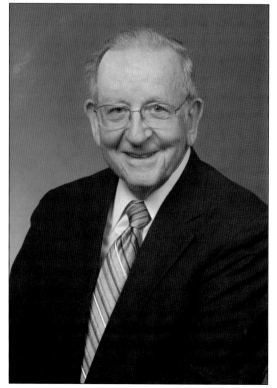

Wayne Gilmore, a longtime resident of Opelousas who died in 2011, was the president of Teche Federal Savings Bank (formerly First Federal Savings and Loan) and served on the board of trustees of the Opelousas General Health System for 40 years. Gilmore was recognized as the Opelousas Citizen of the Year and received the Service to Mankind, Chamber Business Person of the Year, and the Rotary Paul Harris Fellow awards.

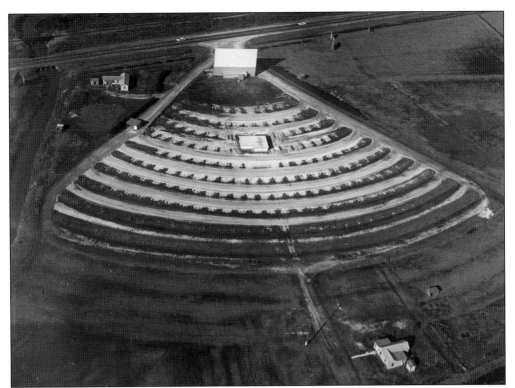

This is an aerial view of the Yam Drive-In Theater, which had a capacity of 300 cars. The theater, designed, built, and owned by E.R. Sellers, was in operation from 1955 until 1975. For two decades, many young couples in Opelousas had their first dates at this drive-in.

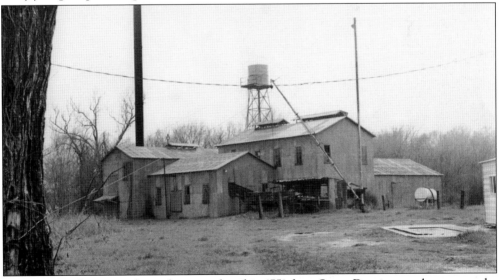

Canne à sucre (sugar cane) was first introduced in 1751 from Santo Domingo and grown on the plantation of the Jesuit order in New Orleans. About 200 years later, in the 1950s and 1960s, the Thistlethwaite Syrup Mill operated in Washington, Louisiana, producing premium cane syrup under the Thisco label. Today, the sugar cane industry contributes $2 billion to Louisiana's economy annually.

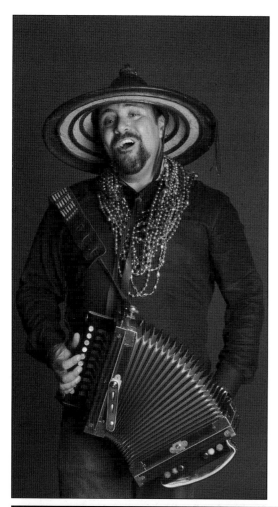

Terrance Simien (left) is an eighth-generation Creole from one of the pioneer Creole families in the Mallet area. He was introduced to music via the piano at home, the Catholic church choir, and his school band program. While in his teens, he taught himself to play accordion and formed his first band, Terrance Simien and the Mallet Playboys. In the early 1980s, Simien was one of only two—Sam Brothers was the other—emerging zydeco artists to perform indigenous zydeco roots music. This was a pivotal time in zydeco music history, as the pioneers of the genre were aging and the music was in jeopardy of dying off without the critical presence of emerging artists perpetuating the traditions. In 2001, Simien and his wife and business partner, Cynthia, created the Creole for Kidz & The History of Zydeco, providing performances to students. The program has reached 500,000 students in more than 20 states, as well as in Mali, the Dominican Republic, Brazil, Paraguay, Canada, and Australia. The Simiens created MusicMatters Inc., a nonprofit artist advocacy and education organization. In 2008, Terrance Simien and the Zydeco Experience was the first ensemble to win a Grammy in the now-defunct Zydeco and Cajun category. Below, in 1991, Simien (left) performs with Paul Simon (center) and C.J. Chenier (right) in the Lafayette Cajundome.

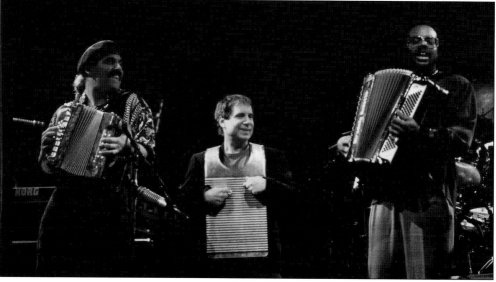

On December 6, 2012, the nominees in the Regional Roots category were announced for the 55th Grammy Awards. Nominees included Le Band Courtbouillon, a trio comprised of Steve Riley, Wayne Toups, and Wilson Savoy, and Cory Ledet, a 31-year-old accordion ace and disciple of Clifton Chenier. Le Band Courtbouillion won the Grammy on February 10, 2013. Seen here in January 1991 at Dr. Barry Ancelet's *cochon de lait* are Dewey Balfa (front), Vance Lanier (left), and Steve Riley (right).

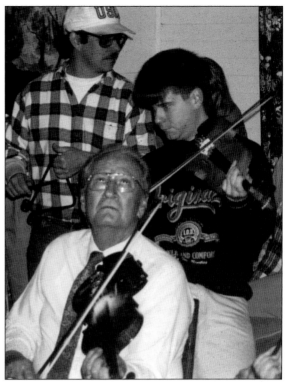

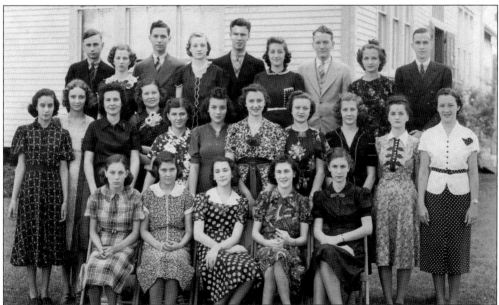

The class of 1938 at Immaculate Conception Academy included, from left to right, (first row) Josephine Veillon, Elaine Soileau, Patricia Fontenot, Carrie Ledoux, and Bernardine Reed; (second row) Catherine Mistric, Jeanne Bertrand, Alma F. Bass, Billie Elder, Mildred Bordelon, Jennie Compton, Mildred Bertrand, Julie Burgin, Frankie Moreau, Edith Broussard, and Doris Bercier; (third row) Roy Breaux, Rita Chachere, Curtis Bertrand, Belle Dubuisson, A.L. Bertrand, Dorothy Edwards, Dick St. Cyr, Edith Hollier, and John Wilkins.

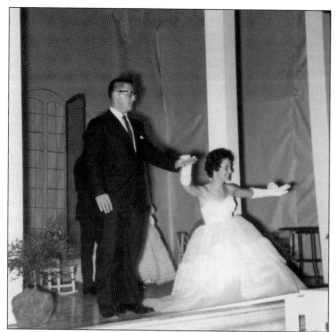

The Mandatory Education Act of 1916 required that English be spoken in schools, thus beginning the Americanization of the area. However, in 1955, the successful, state-sponsored Acadian Bicentennial Celebration became the genesis of the French Renaissance, which led to the teaching of French in the schools by CODOFIL. Seen here in December 1962 are Carroll Richard (left) and Lanell Savoie during the Sunset High School Future Business Leaders Association's coronation dance.

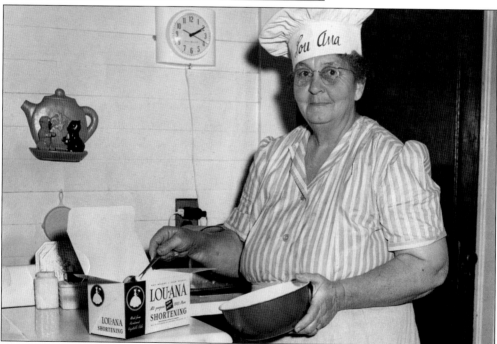

The anonymous *Breaux Manuscript*, the earliest existing local folklore commentary, noted that travelers requiring assistance during bad weather could seek shelter at any door. It also mentions communal projects including the *piocherie* (hoeing party), the *couvrage* (shingling party), the *ramasserie de coton* (cotton harvest), and other demonstrations of community support, all of which are forerunners of modern-day festivals. In the mid-1940s, Aline Richard, seen here, received the LouAna Cook of the Week Award, a contest sponsored by LouAna Foods of Opelousas. (Courtesy of Judi Lucito.)

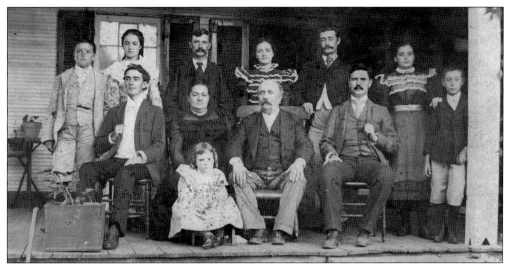

The Pavy family posed for this photograph at their home. They are, from left to right, (seated) Dr. Felix Octave Pavy; Laperle Guidry; Lucille Pavy; Alfred Pavy; and Judge Benjamin Henry Pavy; (standing) Paul David Pavy, the principal of Opelousas High School; Josephine "Josie" Guilbeau, the daughter of Dudley and Blanche Pavy Guilbeau; Pierre Pavy; Louise Pavy, the resident "house mother" at the Southwestern Louisiana Institute (now the University of Louisiana at Lafayette); Raoul Pavy; Lilla Mae Pavy; and Dr. Albert Berchman Pavy.

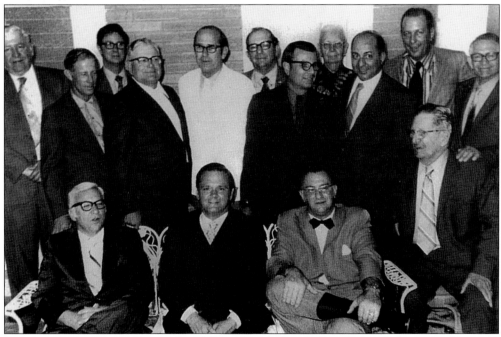

Seen here in the late 1980s are political legends of St. Landry Parish, from left to right, (first row) Sen. Frank Diesi, US Rep. Gillis Long, Rep. Howard B. Dejean, and Sheriff Daly Joseph "Cat" Doucet; (second row) Councilman John Babineaux, Police Juror Cedric Frugé, Eunice mayor Curtis Joubert, Clerk of the Court Harold Sylvester, Councilman Tommy Powell, and Eunice marshal Leonce Bellow; (third row) Deputy Bill Soileau, Sen. Armand Brinkhaus, Sheriff Adler Ledoux, Assessor Lennie Savoy, and Trooper L.B. Carrier.

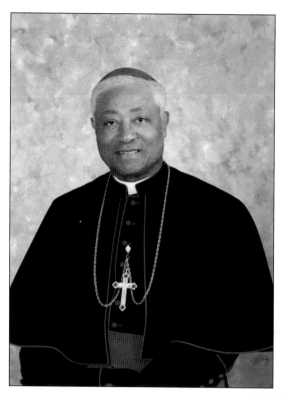

Bishop Dominic Carmon, a native of Opelousas, grew up on a farm in the Gradney (Gradenigo) Island community. He studied at Divine Word seminaries in Mississippi, Illinois, and Iowa, and at DePaul University in Chicago. After being ordained as a priest in 1960, he served as a parish priest in Papua New Guinea, Chicago, and Opelousas. On December 16, 1992, Pope John Paul II appointed him auxiliary bishop of New Orleans, where he continues to serve the church in retirement.

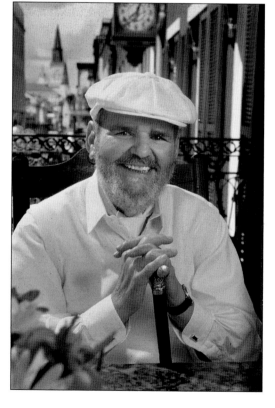

Chef Paul Prudhomme learned the importance of using the freshest ingredients while cooking at his mother's side. His strong curiosity for life motivated him to leave Louisiana in his early 20s and travel across the United States to experience many culinary environments. In July 1979, Prudhomme opened K-Paul's Louisiana Kitchen in New Orleans' French Quarter. In 1983, he created his own line of all-natural spices and smoked meats. Prudhomme has written nine cookbooks, produced six cooking videos, and propelled the distinctive cuisine of his native St. Landry into the international spotlight.

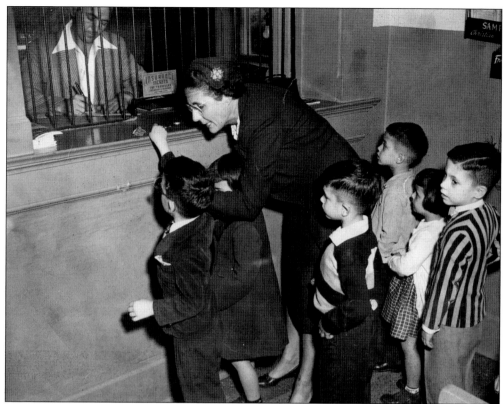

St. Landry people are a colorful group. A sense of humor and adventure are common traits. In 1953, Irene Moise's kindergarten class journeyed to Eunice from Opelousas on their first train trip. Above, the two boys in the right foreground are Chris Dunbar (left) and Tom Bordelon, and Rickey Heck is buying tickets with Moise.

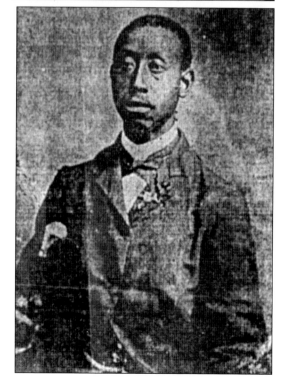

Free people of color, so-called because of mixed blood and heritage, were considered a third race in Louisiana before the Civil War. Some of them even owned businesses, but things changed after the war, when all free people of color were classified as black. On April 22, 1884, John Baptiste Zacharie, seen here, a Creole married to Georgia Reed, was elected constable for the first ward of St. Landry Parish. He was killed in the late 1890s and is buried in St. Landry Cemetery. (Courtesy of Lawrence Zachary.)

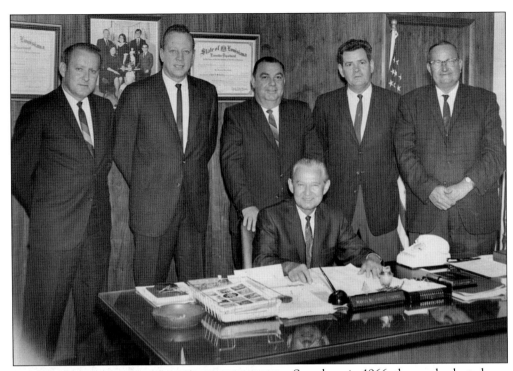

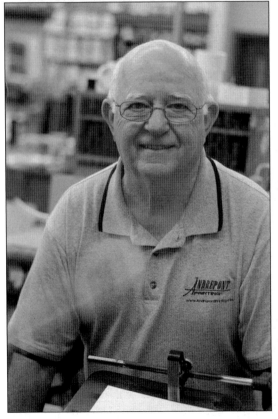

Seen here in 1966, the newly elected Opelousas city council members were (seated) mayor E. Wilfred Cortez, a decorated World War II veteran who served two terms as mayor; (standing, from left to right) Howard Zerangue; Bob Casanova, the mayor pro tem for four years; Vernon Schwartzenburg; Gus Boyd; and Theo Pitre.

Philip Andrepont, the president of Andrepont Printing Inc., was born in Ville Platte in 1942 to Lawrence and Aline Andrepont. He graduated from the Academy of the Immaculate Conception (now Opelousas Catholic) in 1961, where he made honorable mention all-state in football. After leaving the service in 1965, Andrepont began working at his father's printing company. The president of the Opelousas Jaycees and the Yambilee Association, Andrepont is married to the former Debby Randall and has one son, André, and a stepdaughter, Susan Newman.

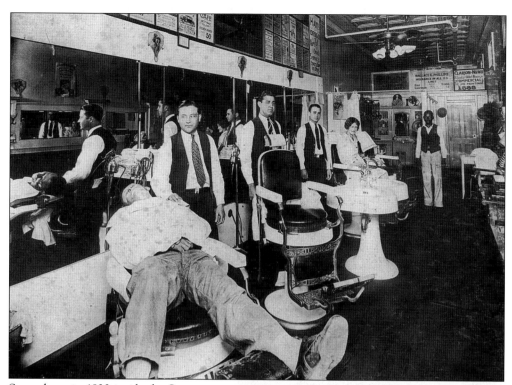

Seen above in 1930 inside the Star Barber Shop, on Landry Street in Opelousas, are, from left to right, barbers Otis Welch, Lee Cormier, and R.J. Cormier. According to Dr. Carl Brasseaux, "St. Landry has a large Creole of Color population because of the parish's position on the western periphery during the community's crucial formative period. The frontier setting afforded Creoles not only the opportunity to acquire cheap land, but also to play a role in forming a frontier society in which they could play a crucial part as a propertied segment of the population."

Laura Balthazar began her employment with the St. Landry Parish sheriff's office in January 1980. She has held the positions of chief criminal deputy and chief civil deputy, becoming the first African American woman in the state to hold both of these top positions. In 2006, following the death of sheriff Howard Zerangue Sr., she served as the interim sheriff.

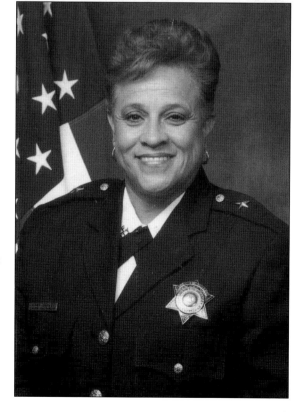

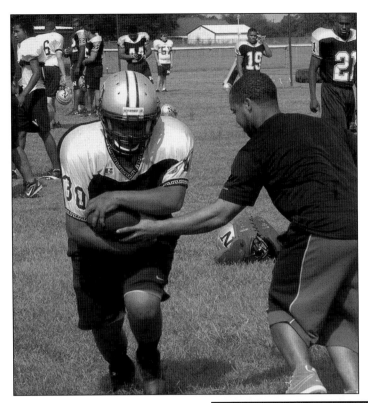

In 2012, members of the Northwest Raiders football team pitched the idea to Brittany Lindon, seen here, of trying out for the team, and she accepted the challenge. Despite being pushed by Raiders head coach Darnell Lee to try kicking, Lindon selected the rugged position of fullback. In 2013, the Acadiana Zydeco, a full-contact woman's football team based in Opelousas, made history by going to St. Louis for its first championship game. (Courtesy of the *Daily World* and Freddie Herpin.)

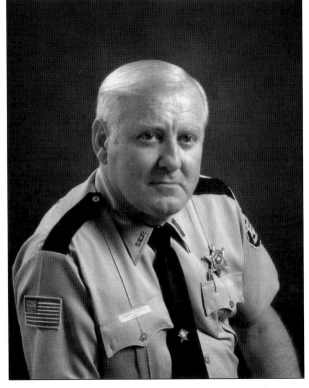

In the 1850s, bands of marauding cattle thieves roamed the countryside. In response, *Comités de vigilance* (vigilante committees) were organized, and the problem soon abated. With a career that culminated in a 26-year term as sheriff of St. Landry Parish, Howard Zerangue Sr. began his work life selling Volkswagens and "bouncing" at the Southern Club before going on to serve as a councilman and the chief of police of the City of Opelousas.

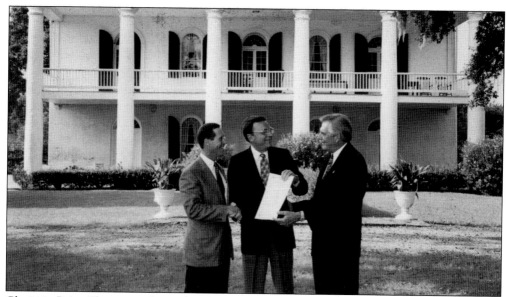

Chrétién Point Plantation, located in Sunset, was originally built by Joseph Chrétién. His son Hypolite married Felicite, who became the overseer of the 640-acre plantation when Hypolite died in 1839. Louis Cornay (center), the former owner of the plantation, is seen here accepting a letter signed by Gov. Edwin Edwards inviting Canadian prime minister Jean Chrétién to visit Louisiana for Franco Féte 1999. The letter was given to Cornay by Carroll Baudoin (right) and Warren A. Perrin (left), then the president of CODOFIL. On September 2, 1995, Chrétién received the Cornays as his guests.

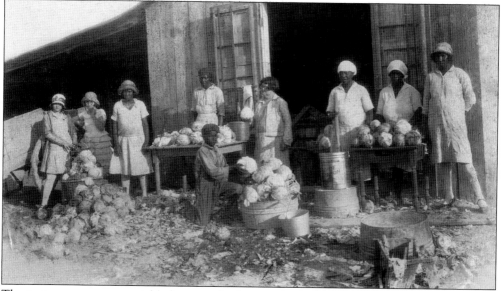

The tasty sweet potato quickly became the favorite food of settlers; however, it has a violent incident in its history. In what is known as the Opelousas Massacre, on September 28, 1868, white terrorists who called themselves "Redeemers" tried to prevent Republicans from winning the fall election in Louisiana. Over a few days, they killed some 200 freedmen, most of whom worked as field hands farming sweet potatoes. This photograph shows field hands working in the parish in 1930. (Courtesy of the Louis V. Bernard Jr. collection.)

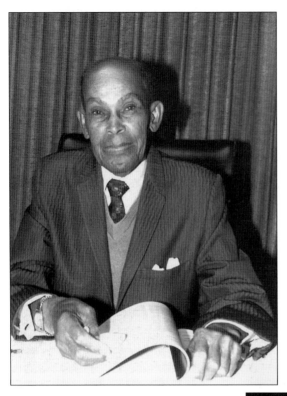

Juneteenth is held annually at the Farmers' Market Pavilion on Landry Street in Opelousas. It is in honor of the events of June 19, 1865, when the last 250,000 slaves in the United States were freed. Today, Juneteenth has come to symbolize for many African Americans what the Fourth of July symbolizes for all Americans: freedom. Dr. August C. Terrence, seen here, who admitted the first patient to Opelousas General Hospital, practiced medicine for 56 years. He served as president of the National Medical Association in 1955–1956 and was a champion of racial equality in medicine.

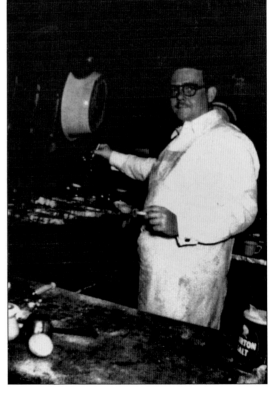

Dr. Ladislas Lazaro II, who founded the St. Landry Clinic in 1921 with Dr. Sidney J. Rozas, was born in Opelousas in 1910 and was known as the "dean of doctors." His father was US Rep. Ladislas Lazaro, so Dr. Lazaro II was educated in Washington, DC. His son Dr. Ladislas Lazaro III, a renowned orthopedic surgeon, died on March 10, 2013. (Courtesy Dr. Ladislas Lazaro III.)

Theresa Singleton is seen here on July 14, 2012, reading to children at a Barnes & Noble bookstore. A librarian by profession, she writes Christian lyrics, poetry, and children's stories. Singleton's first book, *Grandfather Lee & The Bees*, delighted children and taught inspirational life lessons. Her second book, *Zydeco Zoom*, is the story of Zerick, a young Creole boy, and how he deals with his first terrifying musical experience on stage. The book, beautifully illustrated by Laura Foote, introduces children to zydeco culture.

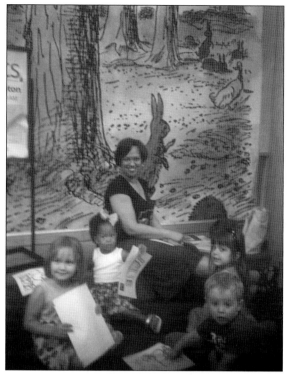

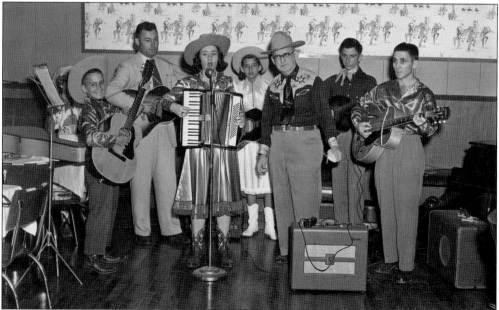

"Rockin' Sidney" Simien, born into a sharecropper's family in Lebeau, was a zydeco musician whose song "My Toot Toot" became a worldwide hit. The Blue Room Gang is seen here performing in 1952 at a 4-H Club party at the A&P store that also aired live on KSLO Radio. The band was created by Felix Dezauche, the owner of Dezauche & Sons feed store, to promote his Red Bird brand of sweet potatoes. From left to right are Rod Bernard, unidentified, Barbara Quebedeaux, Mabel Sonnier, Felix Dezauche, Rene Fontenot, and Albert "Pee-Wee" McCauley.

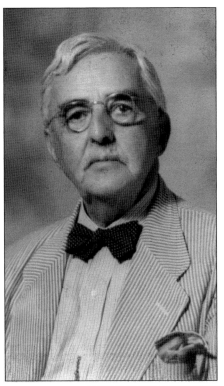

In the early 1900s, three widely grown crops in the area were rice, sugar cane, and cotton. Small-scale farming obligated farmers to engage in seasonal occupations to support their families, including plowing, planting, hoeing, mending fences, and branding cattle. Seen here is Dr. William Robert Lastrapes, who practiced in Opelousas for many years. Many of his patients paid him for his services by bartering produce that they had grown.

August 23, 2012, marked the 100th anniversary of the alleged kidnapping of Bobby Dunbar, a mystery that has fascinated America for over a century. In 2008, National Public Radio's *This American Life* aired an episode about the case. The Dunbars were at their camp near Opelousas when four-year-old Bobby vanished. After searching for him, the parents became convinced the boy was kidnapped. Seen below is the crowd that gathered on April 21, 1913, at the railroad depot to welcome Dunbar home after he was supposedly found. The story was retold, with a unique twist involving DNA testing, in the 2012 book *A Case for Solomon*, written by Bobby Dunbar's granddaughter Margaret Dunbar Cutright and Tai McThenia.

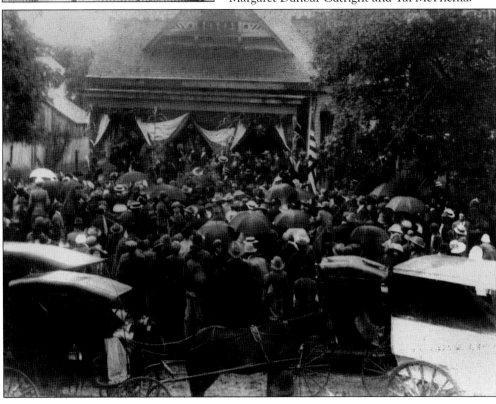

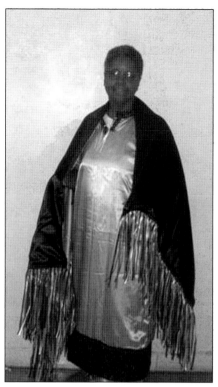

A research project is currently exploring whether plants that older generations relied on for healing might have applications in modern medicine. The project has its origin in the Healer's Garden at Vermilionville. "Most of the knowledge came from native Americans," said University of Louisiana at Lafayette anthropology professor Ray Brassieur, PhD. "The traditional knowledge of local plants was kept alive in Louisiana longer than in other areas of the country because native American groups were not forced to relocate and many still remain here today, like the Attakapas." Mirva Broussard of the Louisiana Attakapas Opelousas Prairie Tribe is seen here.

Desegregation in Louisiana's public schools came slowly. In 1964, the Civil Rights Act outlawed racial segregation, but some parishes took years to comply. By 1967, a total of 30 parishes still had made no arrangements to desegregate. In 1970, a group of 45 parishes were ordered to come up with a plan or risk the loss of federal funding. Louisiana's public schools did not fully integrate until the mid-1970s. The Opelousas Senior High School class of 1937 is seen below in front of the school.

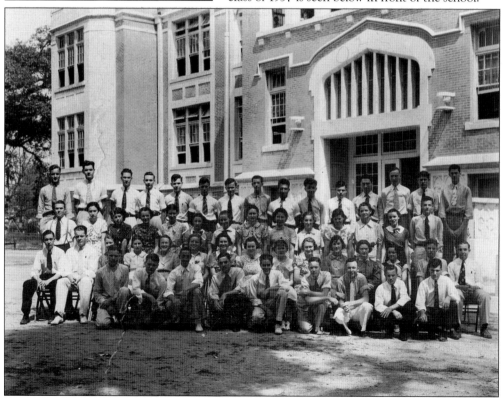

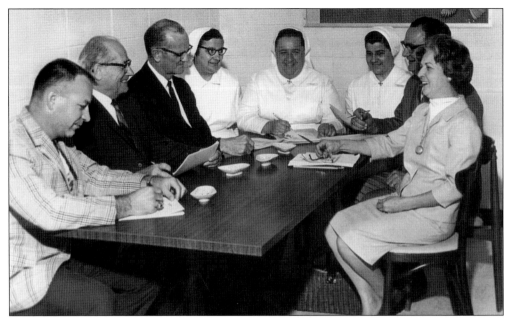

Health care in St. Landry Parish is better now than it has ever been before. Established in May 1957, the Opelousas General Health System has grown into a 256-bed facility offering an extensive variety of specialized services. This early photograph of a board of directors' meeting of the Prompt Succor Nursing Home shows, from left to right, Sam Hamilton, J.Y. Fontenot, Sidney Sandoz Jr., Sr. Dolores Haddad, Sr. Margaret Lafleur, Sr. Benedict Allain, Pat Willis Sr., and Alyce Schermer Couvillion.

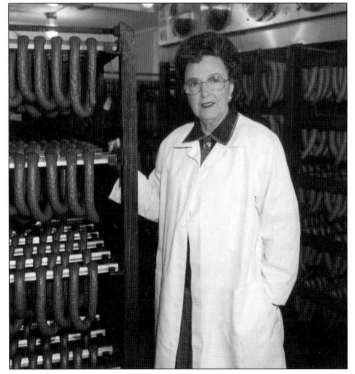

In 1949, Eula (seen here) and Tom Savoie purchased a small grocery store in Opelousas where the family also sold hogs. In 1955, they were unable to sell all of their hogs. Eula's mother, Ezola Morris, suggested that they use her old family recipe and turn the hogs into smoked sausage. Eula took her mother's advice and began selling the sausage in the store. Due to its popularity and consumer demand, she soon began selling it throughout the region. From modest beginnings making only 25 pounds of sausage per week, Eula created a multimillion-dollar enterprise, Savoie's Sausage & Food Products Inc.

Nine

PUBLIC AFFAIRS

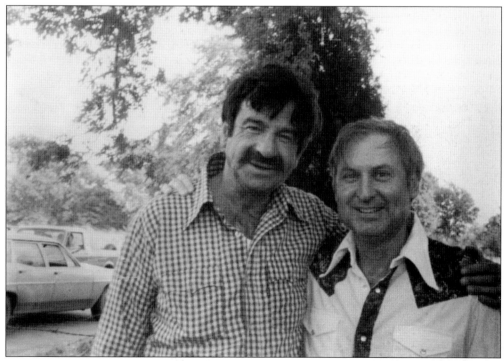

One aspect of the old range days remains unchanged today: the love of horses. When the first settlers arrived, horses and cattle were already in the area. Actor Walter Matthau (left) came to the parish to film the movie *Casey's Shadow*, the story of a Cajun horse trainer who won the national championship Quarterhorse race. The film was shot next door to Morgan Goudeau III's (right) horse farm on the Lewisburg Highway. Matthau loved the area and mentioned on Johnny Carson's *Tonight Show* that Goudeau made him feel welcome.

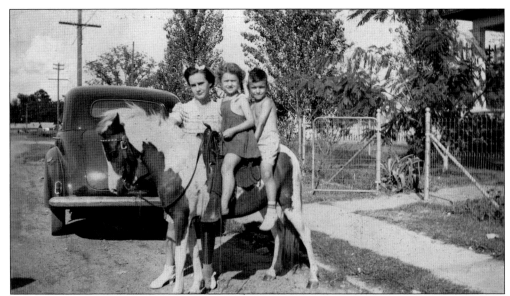

Creole folklorist Rebecca Henry, the daughter of a sharecropper from Leonville, founded the Creole Heritage Folklife Center in Opelousas. Cajuns and Creoles were among the first cowboys participating in some of the earliest cattle drives in the 1770s. Since World War II, Cajun jockeys have won a total of 21 Triple Crown races. Hazel Bernard is pictured here in Opelousas around 1940 with (on horse) an unidentified girl and Gerald Mouton. (Courtesy of the Louis V. Bernard Jr. collection.)

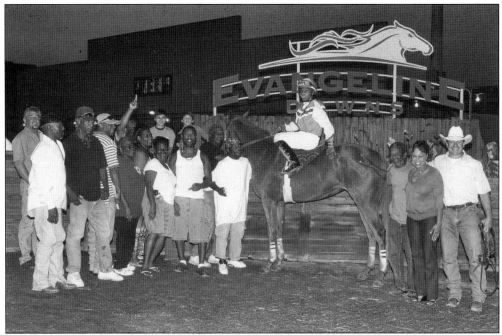

Evangeline Downs Racetrack & Casino, the first "racino" built in this country, features a state-of-the-art facility with a one-mile oval track. The entire property consists of close to 750 acres. The track houses nearly 1,000 stalls on the backside. Thoroughbred horse racing is held there from April 18 to September 8. Seen here on May 20, 2011, is winner Ellen's Lady, owned by Rita Taylor and trained by Donald Taylor, with jockey C.J. McMahon.

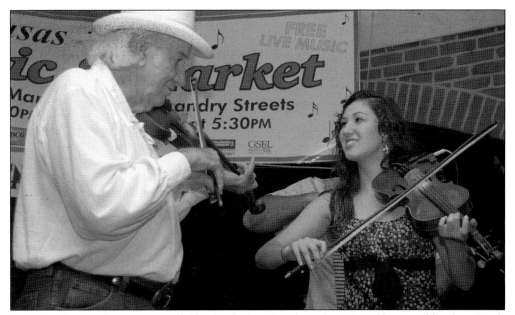

The legendary Hadley J. Castille (left), who died on October 25, 2012, and his granddaughter Sarah Jayde Williams performed at the Music and Market on October 19, 2007. Having been surrounded by music her entire life, it was only natural that Williams would be the fourth generation of the musical Castille clan to play. Initially trained at the age of four as a classical violinist, she soon learned Cajun fiddle from her loving grandfather. Williams became a fine vocalist, singing fluently in both Cajun French and English.

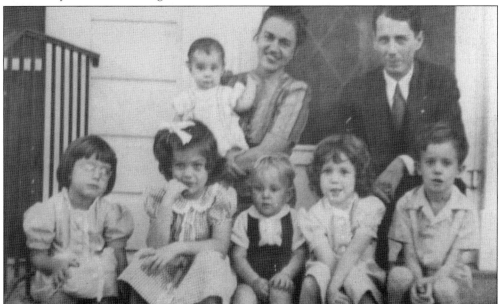

The Fontenot family is seen here in 1944. They are, from left to right, (first row) Lilias, Frances, William, Caroline, and Joseph; (second row) Marie Celeste, Ruth Robertson, and L. Austin Fontenot Jr., who, like his father, was an attorney. In 1943, he moved his family from Washington to Opelousas to be closer to his law office because he could not get enough gasoline rationing tickets to allow for driving from his Washington home to Opelousas. (Courtesy of William and Mary Fontenot.)

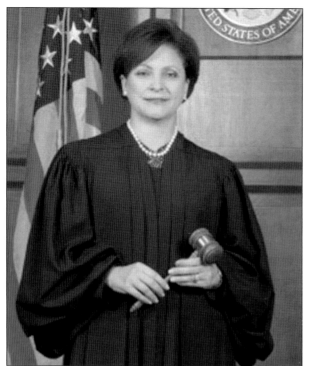

On October 4, 2011, Nannette Jolivette Brown was nominated by Pres. Barack Obama and became the first black woman to serve on the federal bench in Louisiana. Among the many honors Jolivette Brown has received are the 1994 Black Achiever in Business Award and Tulane Law School's Distinguished Minority Graduate Award. In 1985, she received a bachelor of arts in journalism from the University of Louisiana at Lafayette, which honored her with the 2012 Outstanding Alumni Award.

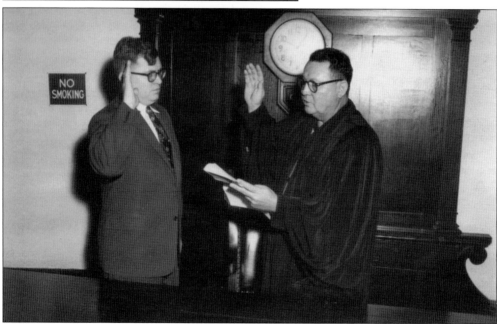

Justice Albert A. Tate Jr. was a long-serving Louisiana judge known for his leadership in the legal profession. He was born in Opelousas to Albert Tate Sr. and the former Adelaide Therry. He received his law degree from Yale Law School in 1947 and served on the Louisiana First (1954–1960) and Third Circuit (1960–1970) Courts of Appeal, the US Fifth Circuit Court of Appeals (1979–1986), and the Louisiana Supreme Court (1958; 1970–1979). Justice Tate (left) is seen here being sworn in to the First Circuit Court of Appeals in 1954 by Judge J. Cleveland Frugé, his uncle.

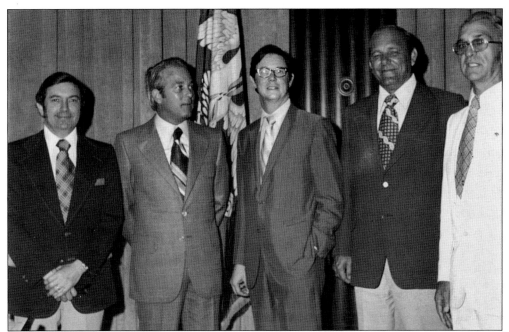

District attorney Austin Fontenot and Sen. Isom Guillory had long associations with US Sen. Huey P. Long Jr., who dominated state politics before being killed on September 9, 1935. Seen here at the governor's office in the early 1970s are, from left to right, Sen. Robert K. Guillory, the son of Isom Guillory and a native of Eunice who was known as the "father of I-49;" Gov. Edwin W. Edwards, Sen. Armand Brinkhaus, Rep. Louis Dischler, and Rep. Steve Dupuis of Opelousas.

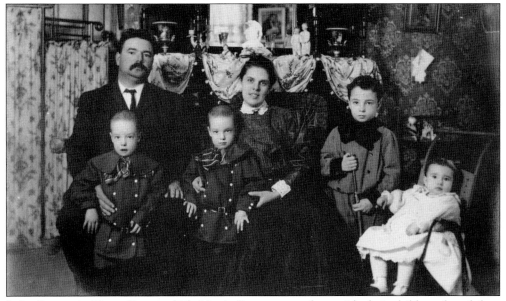

Judge Benjamin Henry Pavy and Ida Veazie Pavy are seen here with their children, from left to right, twins Alfred and Albert, Veazie, and Evelyn. After this photograph was taken, three more children were born: Yvonne Louise, Marie Aline, and Ida Catherine. Judge Pavy was born in 1874 in Couleé Crouche and educated in Opelousas, where he began his law practice in 1901 after having read the law at the office of Edward Veazie, his father-in-law.

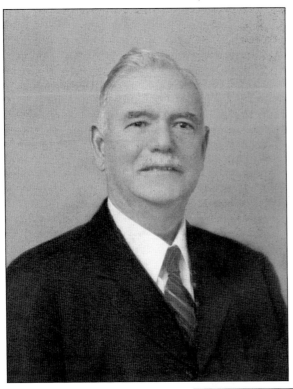

Judge Benjamin Henry Pavy, seen here, was a state district court judge in St. Landry and Evangeline parishes. He was gerrymandered out of office in 1935 through the intervention of his political rival, powerful US senator Huey P. Long Jr. One of Pavy's sons-in-law, Dr. Carl Austin Weiss Sr., was Long's alleged assassin, although the Pavy and Weiss families have long disputed that assertion.

The defense theories advanced by Dr. Donald A. Pavy, the author of *Accident and Deception: The Huey Long Shooting*, are built on affidavits from people who were in the Louisiana capitol the night of the incident. According to Dr. Pavy, Dr. Carl Weiss, who was unarmed at the time, lost his composure after a third, very rough rebuff, screaming at Long and hitting him on the lip. This theory was also supported by the superintendent of the Louisiana State Police, Francis C. Grevemberg, seen here, who had cracked down on the mob's criminal activity and found evidence of a cover-up. (Courtesy of fonvillewinans.com.)

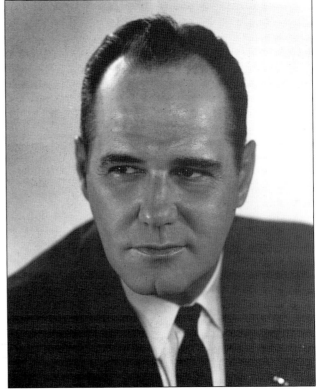

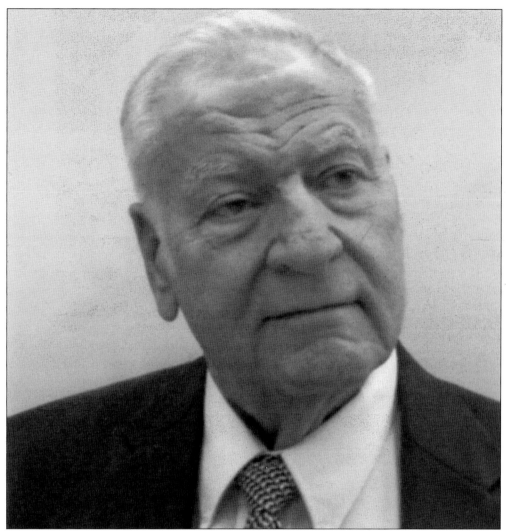

Dr. Pavy, seen here, wrote, "One bodyguard, probably Messina (a nervous type), always close and often in the rear of Huey, pulled his gun, which hung up in the holster and misfired, striking Huey in the back." Pavy is not the first writer to blame a bodyguard for Long's death. Ed Reed, the author of *Requiem for a Kingfish: The Strange and Unexplained Death of Huey Long* (1986), contends that Murphy Roden, who was trained to react immediately, fired at Weiss at close range but his bullet struck Long. Reed opines that Weiss never got close enough to shoot before he was gunned down.

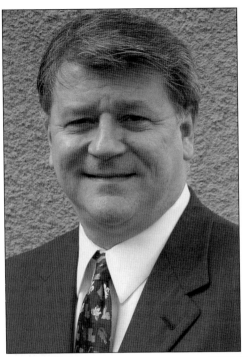

In W. Thomas Angers's 2005 book, *My Wars: Nazis, Mobsters, Gambling and Corruption; Colonel Francis C. Grevemberg Remembers*, Grevemberg confirms, by sworn affidavit, the details of a cover-up by the Bureau of Criminal Investigations in the killing of Long. Angers, seen here, wrote: "The Long machine was under mob protection payoff. If word got out that bodyguards killed Long, followers would turn against the Long machine. If they lost the governorship they would lose the protection money, creating criminal motive for the coverup."

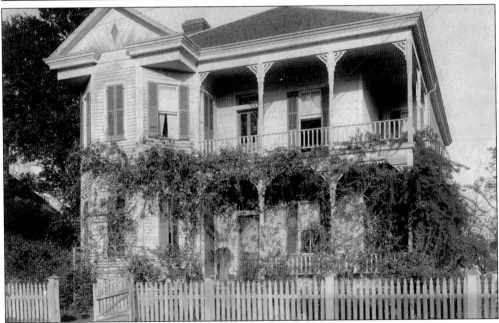

Edith Garland Dupré was born in 1881 in Opelousas, when education for women was at the dawn of acceptance. She graduated in 1900 from Sophie Newcomb Memorial College in New Orleans. In 1901, she joined a faculty of eight who opened the doors of Southwestern Louisiana Institute, now the University of Louisiana at Lafayette. For 43 years, she dedicated her talents to the college, which she helped mold into an accredited institution of higher education. Dupré served as the head of the English department. Seen here in the late 1800s is the house owned by Dupré's father, Laurent Dupré, on Market Street.

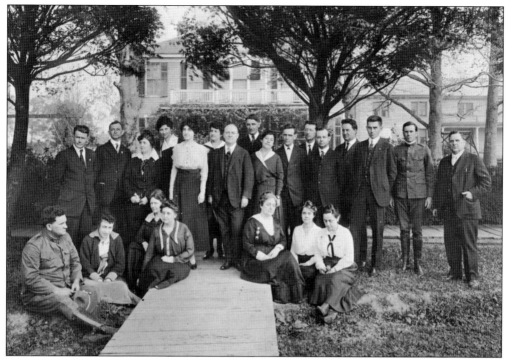

Seen here in 1916 are the members of the faculty at Southwestern Louisiana Institute. Standing in the center is school president Edwin Lewis Stephens, known as the "Father of Southwestern." The two ladies sitting on the right in the first row with white blouses are Hugh McLaurin (left) and Edith Garland Dupré, for whom the Dupré Library was named when it was built in 1962. Dupré was the head of the college's library from 1901 until 1923.

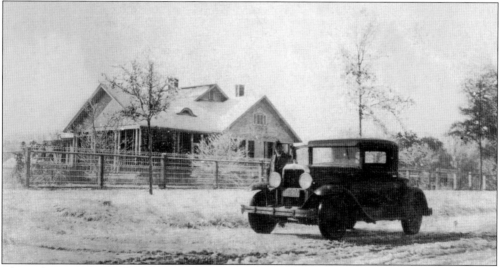

The 1956 Louisiana Mother of the Year, nominated by the Pilot Club, was Opelousas-born Laurence "Betsy" Dupré Pavy, the wife of Dr. Albert Pavy Sr. The Pavys' children all became prominent citizens, including Dr. Robert Pavy, Maj. Laurent Pavy, Dr. Donald A. Pavy, Dr. Albert Pavy Jr., Judge Garland Pavy, attorney Octave Pavy, Jeanne P. Sellers, and Adele P. Comeaux. Dr. Albert Pavy Sr.'s home on Jefferson Street is seen here in 1920.

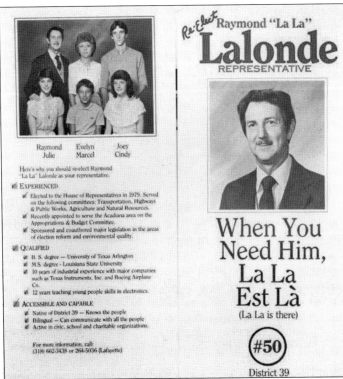

Re-Elect Raymond "La La"

Lalonde
REPRESENTATIVE

Raymond   Evelyn   Joey
Julie   Marcel   Cindy

Here's why you should re-elect Raymond "La La" Lalonde as your representative.

☑ EXPERIENCED

- ☑ Elected to the House of Representatives in 1979. Served on the following committees: Transportation, Highways & Public Works, Agriculture and Natural Resources.
- ☑ Recently appointed to serve the Acadiana area on the Appropriations & Budget Committee.
- ☑ Sponsored and coauthored major legislation in the areas of election reform and environmental quality.

☑ QUALIFIED

- ☑ B. S. degree — University of Texas Arlington
- ☑ M.S. degree - Louisiana State University
- ☑ 10 years of industrial experience with major companies such as Texas Instruments, Inc. and Boeing Airplane Co.
- ☑ 12 years teaching young people skills in electronics.

☑ ACCESSIBLE AND CAPABLE

- ☑ Native of District 39 — Knows the people
- ☑ Bilingual — Can communicate with all the people
- ☑ Active in civic, school and charitable organizations.

For more information, call:
(318) 662-3438 or 264-5036 (Lafayette)

When You Need Him, La La Est Là

(La La is there)

#50

District 39

This is the political card of Rep. Raymond "LaLa" Lalonde, one of the first political candidates to use French phases in campaign literature. In 1984, a well-received advertisement read, "When you need him, 'LaLa' est La." "Buddy" Roemer was governor when Lalonde passed the legislation in the House of Representatives that made Cajuns a certified minority for the purpose of affirmative action. Governor Roemer was upset and feared he would have to veto it. However, the Associated General Contractors Association was in favor of the law, and it was approved.

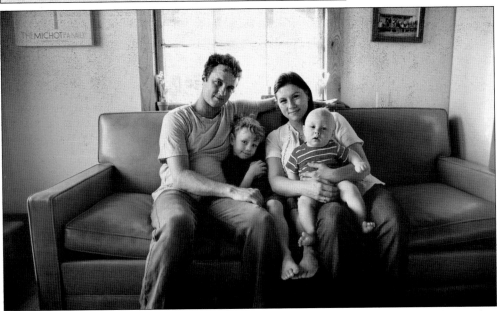

Louis P. Michot is seen here with his wife, Ashlee Michot, and their sons Julien Amedee Michot (left) and Louis Pierce Michot II at their home in Prairie des Femmes, near Arnaudville. Louis plays and produces music with the Lost Bayou Ramblers and Bayou Teche Productions and works with the local brewery, Bayou Teche Brewing. He also founded Acadiana Seed Bank, which retrieves samples of local seeds to preserve for future generations. Ashlee taught Louisiana French at Beau Chene High School.

100

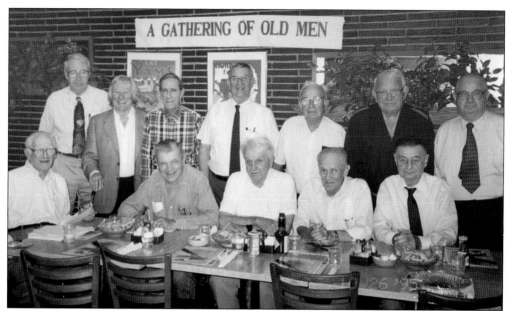

"A Gathering of Old Men," a reunion luncheon held in November 1995 at the Palace Cafe, featured many prominent Opelousians, including, from left to right, (first row) John Thistlethwaite, Hugh Thistlethwaite, Eddie Miller, Tyler Lamson, and Allie B. Perkins; (second row) Ed Burleigh, Alfred Lamson, Paul Manouvrier, Albert Boudreaux, Oren Amy, Sam Chachere, and O.B. Stander.

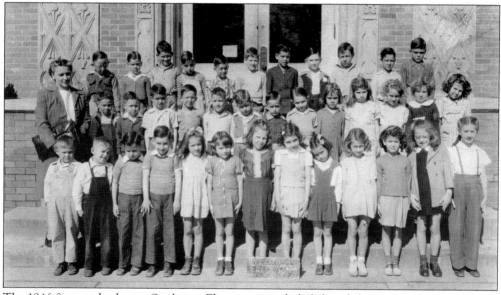

The 1946 first-grade class at Opelousas Elementary included, from left to right, (first row), Moise ?, Dexter Duke, Edward Hollier, Edwin Hollier, two unidentified, Joyce Lanclos, Elaine Ledoux, Sandra Guilbeaux, Ronda Vigi ?, Bernita Wise, Bonnie Richard, Doris Devillier, and ? Perrault; (second row) Vernon ?, Norman Carroll, Frederick Noel, Donald ?, Johnny Stansbury, Roy Mallett, Rodney Bernard, Bill Yates, Betty Lou ?, Elizabeth Boagni, and Evelyn Wyble; (third row) Lyle Fisher, Charles ?, George ?, Elroy Myers, Frank Nezat, Hall ?, Morris Cortez, Larry Stute, Eugene Thibodeaux, Bernard Peck, and Alfred Tinnmons. (Courtesy of the Louis V. Bernard Jr. collection.)

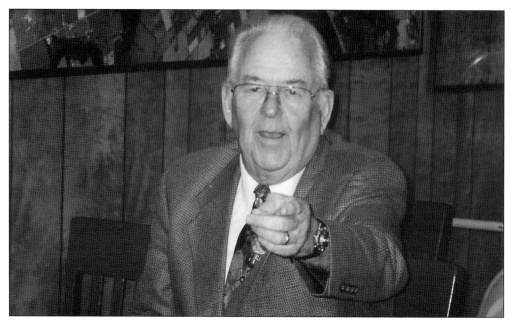

Sunset mayor John L. Olivier is seen here in 2001 presiding over a town council meeting at Sunset City Hall. Olivier served as mayor for 44 years, from 1958 to 2002, setting the record as the longest-serving mayor in the state. Born in 1929 and elected in 1957 at age 28, Olivier was the youngest mayor in the state for many years. An attorney from Sunset, he also served on the CODOFIL board for nearly 20 years and was a dedicated leader in the French Renaissance.

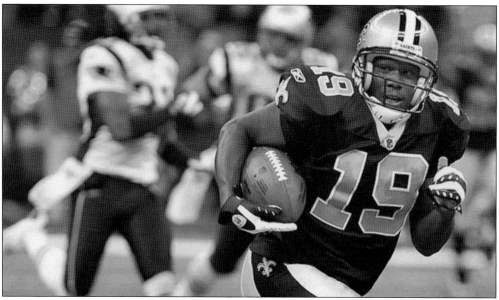

Devery Henderson Jr., a former New Orleans Saints receiver, caught two very memorable passes. On November 9, 2002, Henderson, a native of Opelousas, caught a multiple-tipped pass from LSU quarterback Marcus Randall and scored a touchdown that was dubbed the "Bluegrass Miracle" because it took place in Kentucky. Later, on October 7, 2012, New Orleans Saints quarterback Drew Brees, on a 40-yard touchdown pass to Henderson, made history by throwing a touchdown pass in 48 consecutive games, breaking a record set by Johnny Unitas in 1960.

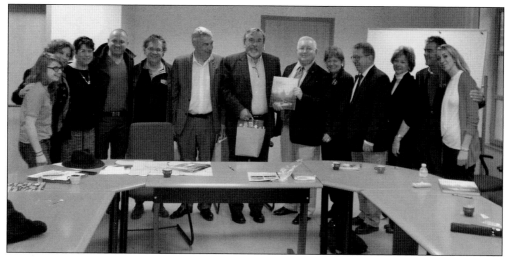

In 2004, in the Brittany region of France, a group called Les Articulteurs formulated a methodology of job creation using arts as a conduit for the promotion of business, culture, and education. With the aid of the consul general of France, Jean-Claude Brunet, a group from St. Landry went to France in October 2012 to meet with their French counterparts. They are, from left to right, Marie Hortense Charier, Celeste Gomez, Jill Hackney, George Marks, Marco Felex, Bernard Vighetti, unidentified, Bill Fontenot, Mavis Frugé, unidentified, Sue Brignac, Charles Jagneaux, and unidentified.

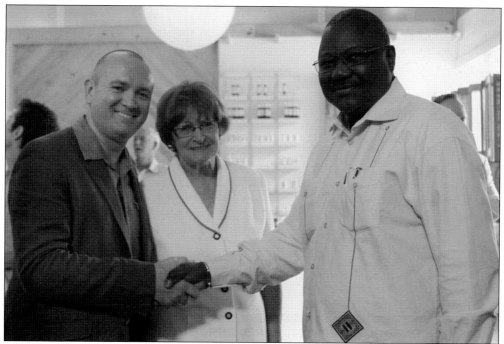

In April 2013, NUNU Arts and Culture Collective hosted a team of 60 visitors from France for the first La Semaine Francais d'Arnaudville summit, which featured talks about creative place, the novel idea of making a partnership among artists, businesses, and politicians. Seen here on August 24, 2012, are, from left to right, George Marks, Mavis Frugé, and Ambassador Filippe Savadogo, the permanent observer of La Francophonie to the United Nations from Burkino Faso.

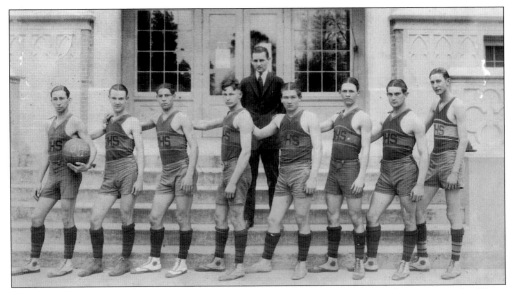

Tony Chachere's Creole Foods began in 1972 as a retirement hobby for south Louisiana chef Tony Chachere. That year, he published *Cajun Country Cookbook*. In 1980, Chachere semiretired (again) at age 75, leaving the operations to his son Alex and his grandson Don. In October 2012, Tony Chachere's Famous Creole Cuisine announced the release of its newest product, Bold Seasoning. Tony Chachere is on the far right in this photograph of the Opelousas High School basketball team. With him are, from left to right, T.H. Littell, Rupert Lyons, Henry Pitre, Lee Garland Jr., Leon Tujaque, Havelin Haw, and Ivan Holman.

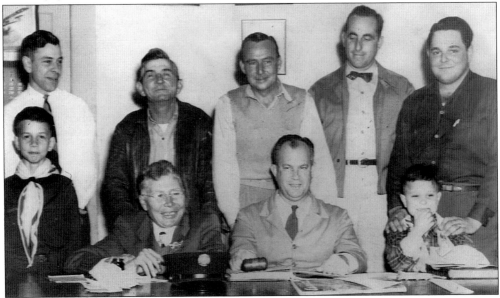

The parish has survived many tragedies. The deadliest natural disaster was the flu pandemic of 1918, which took the lives of many young adults. When fire protection became a priority, Hope, Hook and Ladder Company No. 1, the predecessor to the Opelousas Fire Department, was formed in 1871. These members are, from left to right, (first row) Kenneth Eugene "Gene" Bourdier, Johnny Haas, Bill Bourdier Sr., and Michael Jarrell; (second row) Earl Briggs, Curley Vidrine, Charles Mayer, Bill Johnson, and Jerrell Fontenot.

Rev. Francis J. Coco, SJ, was a popular Jesuit priest who spent 25 years in south Louisiana working as a retreat director at Our Lady of the Oaks Retreat House in Grand Coteau. Being an excellent clarinet player, he had a "music ministry." He also played his clarinet in New Orleans, performing with some of the best jazz musicians in Louisiana, including Pete Fountain, Al Hirt, and Ronnie Kole. The uniqueness of his calling as a clarinet-playing Jesuit priest enabled him to connect to many people whom few others could reach. His biography, *Blessed Be Jazz*, was written by Trent Angers. (Courtesy of Trent Angers.)

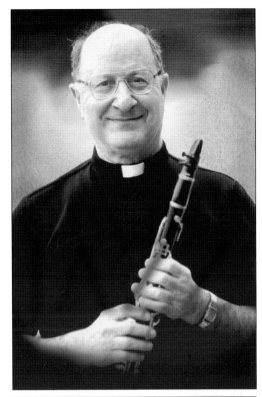

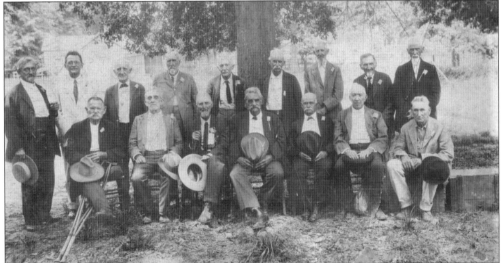

Famous Union general William Tecumseh Sherman, the first president of LSU, was married to Ellen Ewing, a devout Catholic who bore him eight children. Thomas, the oldest son, became a Jesuit priest and baptized General Sherman on his deathbed. Fr. Thomas Sherman died in 1933 and, ironically, is buried in the Jesuit cemetery in Grand Coteau next to Fr. John Salter, SJ, the grandnephew of the vice president of the Confederacy, Alexander H. Stephens. Seen here is a 1925 reunion of St. Landry Parish Civil War veterans, including, in no particular order, Charles Hollier, H.J. Daigle, Henri Chachere, Jim Chachere, Emery Duncan Fisher Sr., and Napoleon Bonaparte Amy.

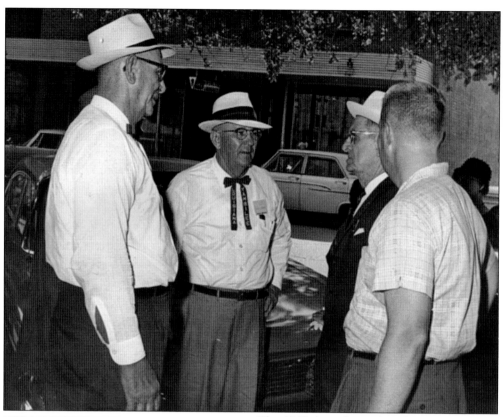

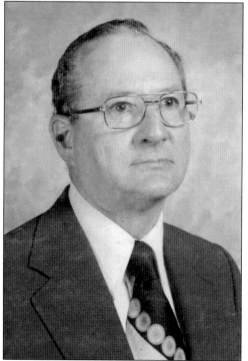

The 1960s brought profound divisiveness to the area. Many young people adopted political views influenced by anti–Vietnam War protests, often causing family splits. Seen above in the 1960s near the St. Landry Parish Courthouse are community leaders (from left to right) Evrard Brown, Octave Fontenot, Sheriff "Cat" Doucet, and Jack Womack. Doucet, running as a Huey Long Democrat, was elected in 1936 and emerged as a colorful, controversial political figure.

Lawrence B. Sandoz Jr., who practiced law for 60 years, was married to Romayne "Plum" Fontenot. Under Gen. George C. Patton, he was one of the youngest majors in the Army. Sandoz was a member of the Louisiana State Bar Association and the editor-in-chief of the Louisiana Law Review. He was also the organizer and chairman of the board of First Acadiana National Bank (now Chase Bank). He did considerable pro bono work and was an advisor to young lawyers.

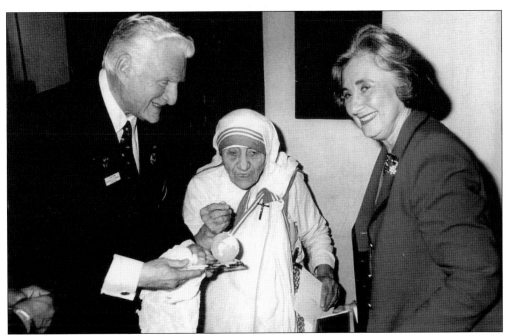

The Fontenots, who came to the area in the mid-1700s, make up the largest family group in the parish. Most descend from Jean-Louis dit Colin Fontenot, a sergeant in the French forces who was stationed in Mobile. Herbert Brown (left) is seen here with his wife, Diane Fontenot Brown (right), and the famous Mother Teresa (center) of Calcutta. A native of Opelousas, Brown is an entrepreneur and philanthropist who developed businesses all over Acadiana. As the president of Rotary International, he also visited 85 countries.

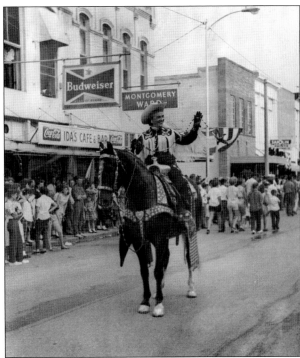

Hazel Perkins and her husband, Oswald, owned Perkins Jewelry Store on Main Street in downtown Opelousas. Hazel rode in the Yambilee parade every year dressed in elaborate garb and riding atop a flashy silver saddle. The crowds in attendance always enjoyed the extravagant display.

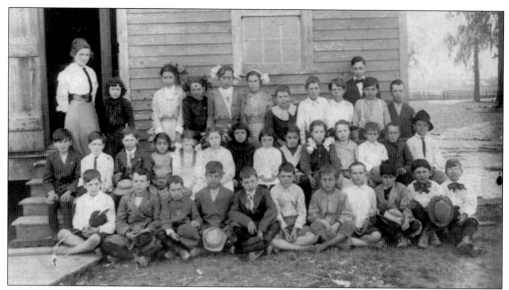

A teacher and her students are seen here in the early 1900s in front of their schoolhouse in Prairie Ronde. In the 1930s, the Works Progress Administration began a free lunch project for school students. After World War II, rural schools established canning centers to aid local residents in preserving foods and cutting and wrapping meats, eliminating the need for *boucheries* (butcheries), which were traditionally held weekly by many rural families.

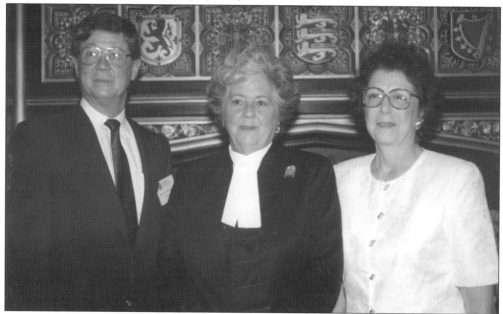

Margaret Brinkhaus, the wife of Sen. Armand Brinkhaus, learned the ways of making jelly as a young girl. After picking berries with her mother and grandmother, she would help with the canning. Her La Caboose Bed & Breakfast was inspired by the original red Southern Pacific Railroad caboose her husband gave to her, along with a typical Cajun cabin converted into a kitchen. She is a founding member of the Louisiana Crafts Guild. Margaret Brinkhaus (right) is seen here with Sen. Armand Brinkhaus and the Hon. Betty Boothroyd in 1992 at the Speaker's House in London's Westminster Palace.

The LHC Group began in 1994 when a group of St. Landry Parish residents saw the community's need for a home health agency. With Ginger Myers (right) as the first nurse, St. Landry Home Care was born. Today, under the leadership of CEO Keith Myers (left), LHC Group cares for nearly 90,000 patients in 23 states. The company remains true to its hometown roots and its motto: "It's all about helping people."

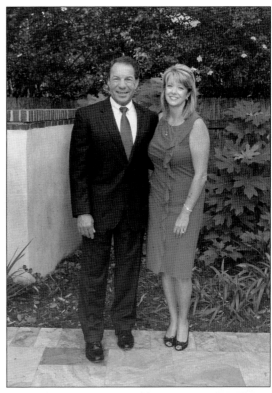

Opelousas police chief Perry Gallow (pictured), who joined the Opelousas Police Department at age 24, has served as the department head since 2007. During his distinguished career, he has been a positive influence on the community and has joined forces with community organizations like the Boys & Girls Club to educate and encourage young people and guide them away from crime and poverty.

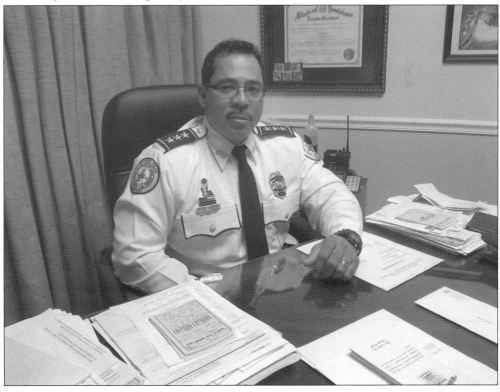

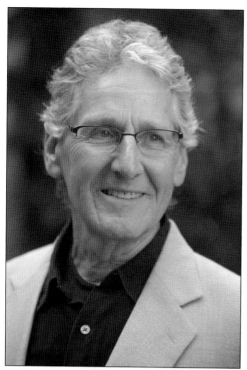

Darrell Bourque, PhD, grew up in a rural community near Sunset. He obtained degrees from the University of Southwestern Louisiana (now the University of Louisiana at Lafayette) and Florida State University. He is now a professor emeritus of English at UL. In 2007, he was appointed the Louisiana poet laureate by Gov. Kathleen Blanco, and was reappointed by Gov. Bobby Jindal in 2009. He serves on the board of the Ernest J. Gaines Center at UL and is the president of the board of the Festival of Words Cultural Arts Collective. In 2013, to critical acclaim, he released *Megan's Guitar and Other Poems from Acadie*, a collection of poems inspired by the Acadian diaspora.

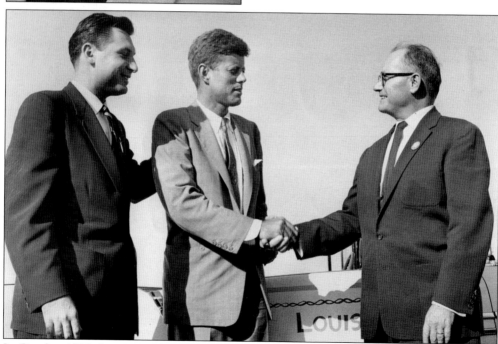

In October 1956, future president John F. Kennedy (center) rode in the Yambilee parade. He was a US senator from Massachusetts at the time and was in Louisiana campaigning for Adlai Stevenson. Morgan J. Goudeau III (left), then an assistant to District Attorney J.Y. Fontenot (right), welcomed Kennedy after he arrived at Opelousas Airport. Goudeau, as campaign manager of the Democratic Party in St. Landry Parish, had arranged the visit.

Ten

SOCIAL LIFE

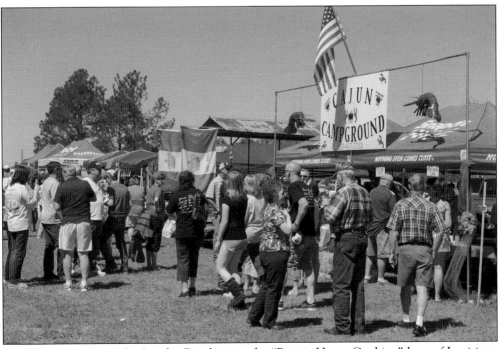

From boudin to yams, St. Landry Parish is on the "Prairie Home Cooking" loop of Louisiana Culinary Trails. It is also home to the Bayou Teche Brewery, featuring its own brand of craft beers that complement the region's local cuisine. In 1986, the Lion's Club of the town of Port Barre began a festival celebrating cracklins, which are *gratons* (fried pork rinds). This photograph from March 25, 2012, shows booths selling crawfish étouffée at the Eunice World Championship Crawfish Étouffée Cook-Off.

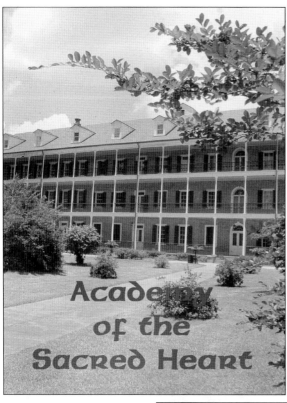

Academy
of the
Sacred Heart

The Grand Coteau National Historic District, listed in the National Register of Historic Places in 1980, features over 70 properties of architectural or historic significance. Creole, French, Acadian, Anglo-American, and Victorian styles are present in the many historic homes, commercial buildings, and religious institutions. The district is one of the few primarily rural historic districts in the United States. Seen here is the Academy of the Sacred Heart (c. 1821), situated on property donated by Mary Sentee, the widow of Charles Smith, which is the second-oldest institute of higher learning for women west of the Mississippi River.

Bishop Michael Jarrell was born in Opelousas, one of four children of William Jarrell Sr. and Jessie Rosa Barnett Jarrell. On June 3, 1967, he was ordained in the priesthood. His ministry included serving as associate pastor at St. Michael Church in Crowley and as pastor of Sacred Heart Church in Broussard and Sacred Heart Church in Ville Platte. In 1993, Bishop Jarrell was ordained to the episcopacy and installed as the second bishop of the Diocese of Houma-Thibodaux. In 2002, he was installed as the sixth bishop of the Diocese of Lafayette. (Courtesy of Jay Falgout Photography.)

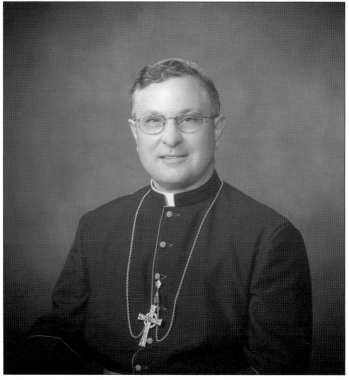

State senator Austin J. Fontenot was a school board member, businessman, banker, farmer, and civic leader in Opelousas. He was a partner or owner of many businesses in the Lewisburg, Church Point, Arnaudville, and Breaux Bridge areas, including Austin's Men & Boys Store, and Fontenot & Guidry Department Store. As a state senator, he was an ardent promoter of commercial and farming interests in St. Landry Parish.

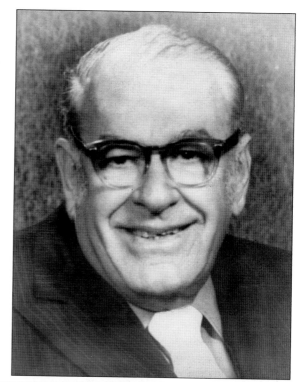

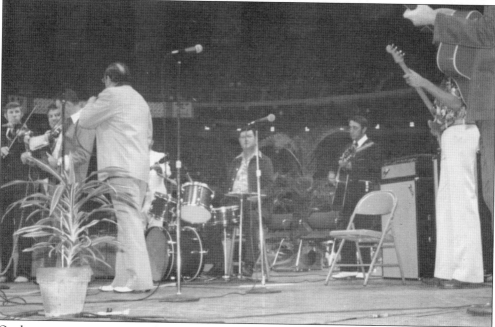

Opelousas musicians are seen here playing Cajun and country and western music at the official dedication and grand opening of the Louisiana Superdome in New Orleans on August 3, 1975. They are, from left to right, Hadley J. Castille, one of the greatest exponents of south Louisiana Cajun fiddle music and a promoter of the French culture; Merlin Fontenot; sheriff Adler Ledoux; Nolan Badeaux; District Judge Robert Brinkman; Jeff Guidry; and Harold Fontenot.

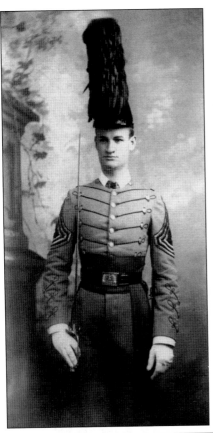

Edward Benjamin Dubuisson graduated from the Virginia Military Institute in 1887. In 1925, he built the Dubuisson Home on Court Street. Elected as district attorney of the St. Landry and Acadia parishes in 1891 at 27 years of age, Dubuisson first married Ann Watts, the daughter of Civil War hero Gen. Owen Watts. After her death, he married Rosa Lastrapes Dupre, with whom he had 10 children.

The house below, on Vine Street in Opelousas, made national news in the early 1940s when it was constructed in a record nine days from start to finish without the use of any power tools. Seen here from left to right are the carpenters, Clyde Perry and Eddie W. Richard, the unidentified new homeowners, and C.B. Deville, a local contractor and the owner of Deville's Lumber Company.

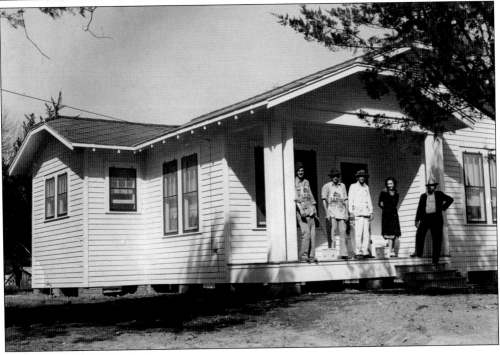

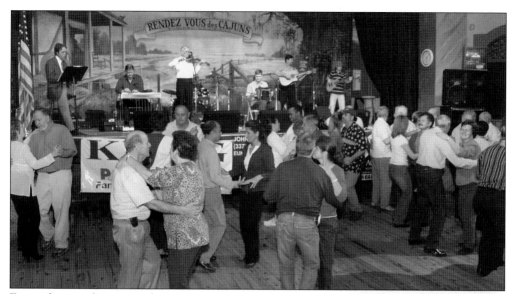

Eunice has two listings in the National Register of Historic Places: the Liberty Theater (c. 1924), an old movie theater that has been restored and is now the Liberty Center; and the Midland Branch Railroad Station (c. 1894), which was converted to the Eunice Museum in 1984. Seen here is the 1,000th performance of *Rendezvous des Cajuns* at the Liberty Center on February 24, 2007, featuring the legendary Elton "Bee" Cormier and the Church Point Playboys, who were the original opening band for the first show, on July 11, 1987. The dancers in the left foreground are Moisey and Louella Baudoin of Erath.

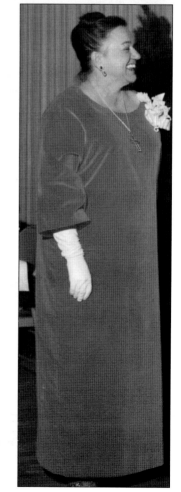

Opelousas native Ruth Robertson Fontenot is seen here in 1971. A local genealogist, historian, and accomplished artist, Fontenot also owned several historic St. Landry Parish homes, including the de la Morandiere House in Washington, the old Governor's Mansion, and Ringrose Plantation, now called the Michel Prudhomme House, in Opelousas. (Courtesy of the family of Ruth Robertson Fontenot.)

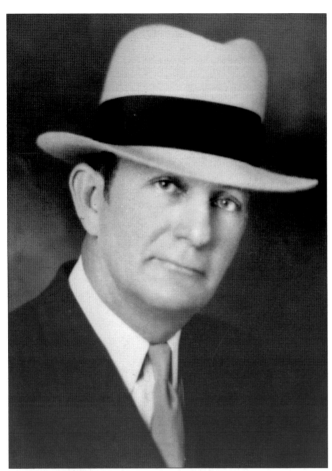

Toby Veltin, a renowned restaurateur, opened several establishments in the Opelousas area, one of which, the Cedar Lane Club, remains in the memories of many today.

In 1925, William J. Sandoz wrote, "That Opelousas was already a center of population and the chief trading post of that vast domain lying between the Atchafalaya River and the Sabine River as early as 1776 there can be no doubt, so that when the framers of the Declaration of Independence were in session at Philadelphia, the early settlers . . . had established their town." Irene E. Shute is seen below riding a mule in downtown Opelousas.

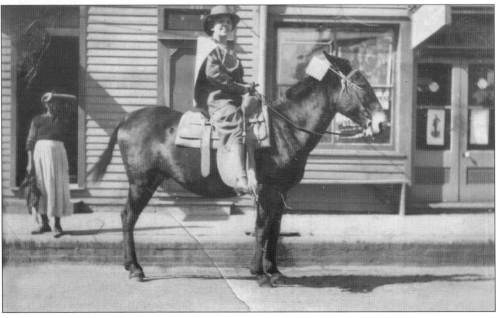

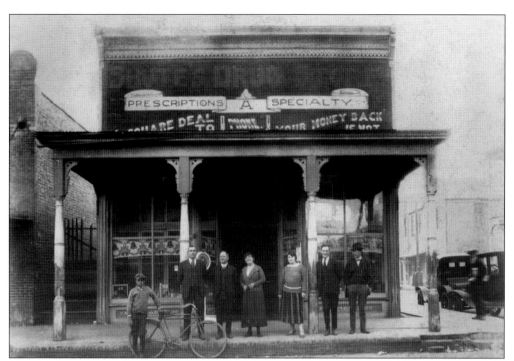

This 1930 photograph shows Irene Shute (center) and others in front of Shute's Drug Store. Today, there are 25 pharmacies in the Opelousas area, with its center at the junction of Interstate 49 and Highway 190.

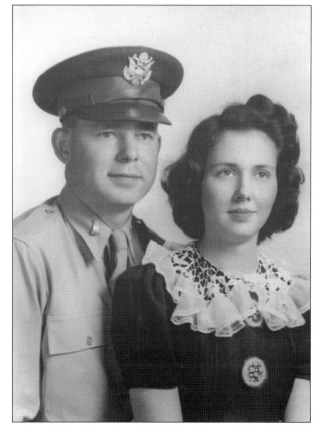

Murray L. Rabalais (left) and Seola Morrow Rabalais of Arnaudville are seen here. Seola was a teacher at Leonville High School until her death in 1965 at the age of 45. Murray taught agriculture at Arnaudville High School until about 1951, when he was appointed the principal in Leonville, where he served until 1963. He then was appointed as the assistant superintendent of St. Landry Parish schools, a position he held until his retirement in 1973.

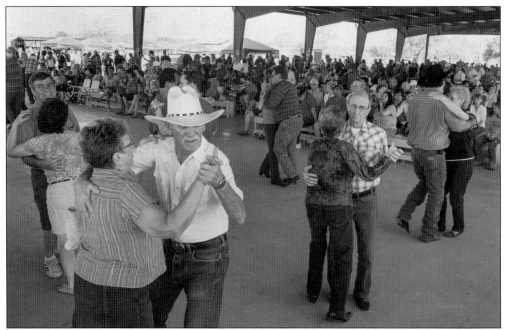

While crawfish is enjoyed throughout Louisiana, it is celebrated in St. Landry Parish. More than merely nourishment, the crawfish is a symbol of the region. By tradition, mounds of the boiled 10-legged crustaceans are piled in the center of a family table so that everyone is able to converse throughout the meal. Here, dancers under Eunice's Northwest Community Center Pavilion celebrate the popular Crawfish Étouffée Cook-Off, begun in 1985.

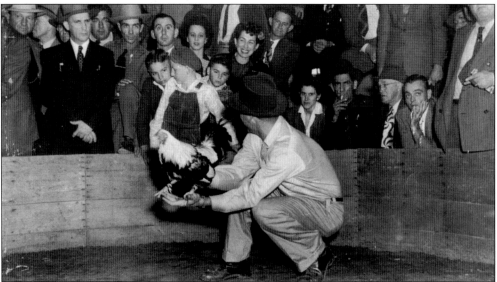

Many fighting gamecocks started life as ordinary roosters. If they showed signs of a fighting spirit, the owner put them into training by making them climb up an incline. Though they had sharp spurs that were lethal, on fighting days, most were fitted with artificial spurs called gaffs. Before they became illegal in 2008, many enjoyed the communal atmosphere found in *batailles de gaimes* (cockfights), exemplified by Cormier's (later Jay's Lounge and Cockpit) in Cankton. Locals participated in such events year-round except during Lent.

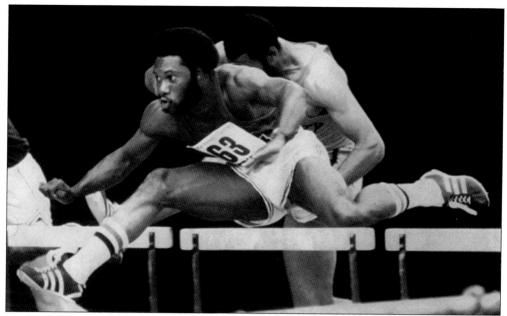

In the early 1970s, Rodney "Rod" Milburn Jr. dominated the 110-meter hurdles, tying the world record three times. After going through 1971 undefeated and winning the 110-meter hurdles event at the 1971 Pan American Games, the Opelousas athlete earned the nickname Hot Rod and was awarded the Track & Field News Athlete of the Year award. At the 1972 Summer Olympics in Munich, Germany, Milburn won the gold medal in the 110-meter hurdles, tying the world record of 13.2 seconds.

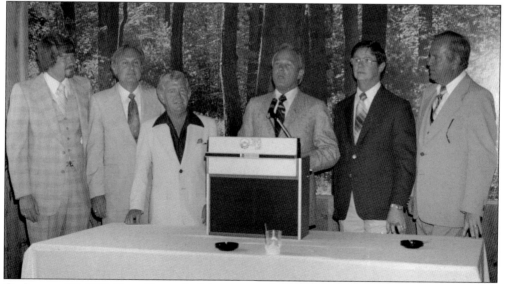

On January 26, 1861, Gov. Alexander Mouton presided over the state's Secessionist Convention. His first wife, Zelia Rousseau, was the daughter of Judge Lucius Jaques Dupré of Opelousas, which was the capital of the state from May 1, 1862, until January 23, 1863. Seen here at Toby's Little Lodge in Opelousas at a fundraiser for Gov. Edwin Edwards's first gubernatorial campaign in 1971 are Morris Weinstein, Morgan J. Goudeau III, Manny Veltin, Edwards, Sen. Armand Brinkhaus, and Lafayette mayor Kenny Bowen.

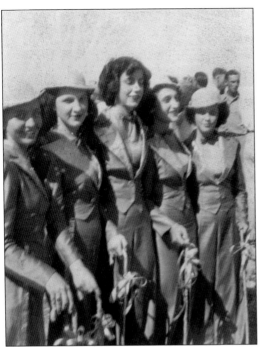

The St. Landry Parish Airport was constructed by the US government as a military airport. In April 1942, a parish bond election passed authorizing $100,000 to purchase property for the airport's construction. In 1947, the first Yamettes are seen here at the St. Landry Parish Airport greeting "Mr. Yam," Charles Mikel. They are, from left to right, Dona Claire Hebert Clary, Betty Jane Goudeau Wolfe, Lorraine Clary Bertinot, Charlene Garbo, and Mary Lou Lott.

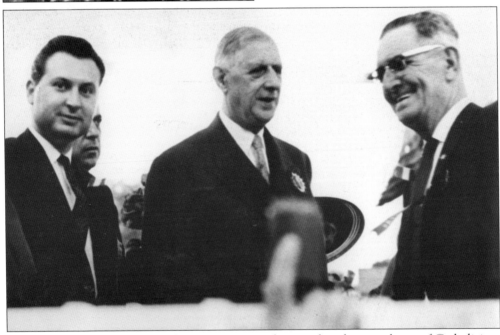

Enmity between the races was always apparent in the area, but the prevalence of Catholicism, which spoke out against racial intolerance, buffered relations somewhat. However, blacks were still discouraged from registering to vote. Catholicism also impeded Ku Klux Klan activity, as the Klan was anti-Catholic as well as anti-black. Seen here in New Orleans on April 26, 1960, are, from left to right, Morgan J. Goudeau III, French president Charles De Gaulle, and Sheriff D.J. "Cat" Doucet. Goudeau and Doucet, early supporters of the Civil Rights Act of 1964, were appointed by New Orleans mayor "Chep" Morrison to be on President De Gaulle's welcoming committee.

Opelousas native Don Cravins Jr., a practicing attorney since 1998, was elected to the Louisiana House of Representatives in 2004, at which time he and his father, Sen. Don Cravins Sr., made Louisiana history by becoming the first father and son to serve simultaneously in the Louisiana legislature. The younger Cravins is now an adjunct professor at George Washington University, where he teaches prosecution and litigation in intellectual property and serves as the chief of staff for US Sen. Mary L. Landrieu in Washington, DC.

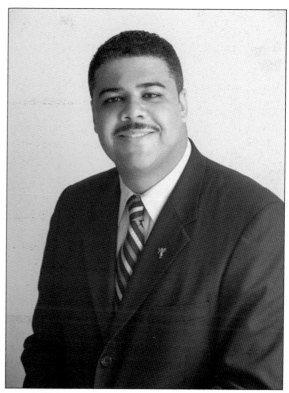

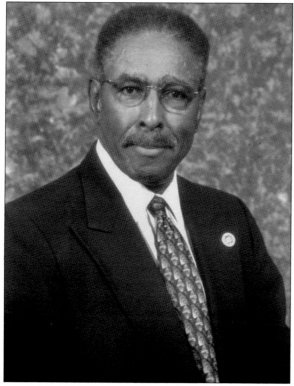

For more than 30 years, Rep. Charles Hudson, seen here, contributed to his state and his community in education, government, and administration. In an email to the authors of this book on August 27, 2012, renowned historian Dr. Carl Brasseaux, a native of St. Landry Parish, wrote, "The parish reflected in microcosm the state as a whole. In the 19th century, the African American population—as a percentage of the total state population—was much higher than it is now. The 19th century political observers always eagerly anticipated the St. Landry election returns because they constituted the most accurate indicator of statewide electoral trends."

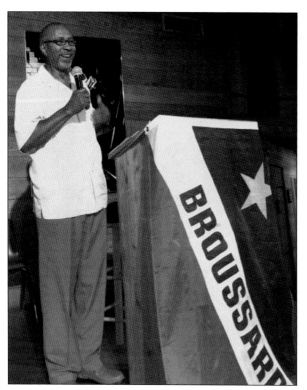

The program *Zydeco est pas salé*, on the University of Louisiana at Lafayette's KRVS 88.7 FM, is a successful effort to preserve Creole heritage by Melvin Caesar and John Broussard, seen here, the first African American named as a commissioner for the USDA Farmers Home Administration. On May 11, 2013, Broussard was the master of ceremonies for the Broussard family reunion in Vermilionville, where the historic Amand Broussard house was rededicated.

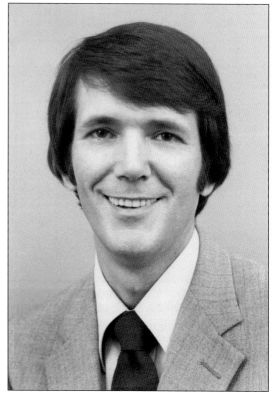

Five courthouses have stood on the courthouse square in Opelousas, the seat of local government since 1806. In 2010, a St. Landry Parish jury awarded Louisiana more than $257 million in a verdict that punished Johnson & Johnson for defrauding the state's Medicaid system. "This verdict sent a message to drug companies that if you give your word to the federal government, you should keep your word," said attorney Patrick Morrow of the firm of Morrow, Morrow, Ryan & Bassett. Seen here is John Michael Morrow Sr., a founding partner of the prominent law firm.

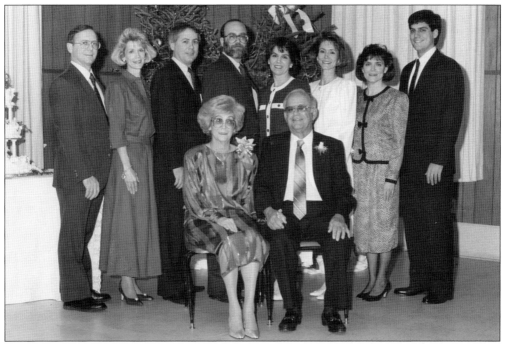

Dr. Robert Louis Morrow (seated, right) was born in 1917 in Arnaudville and died in 1996. The son of Francois Penn Morrow and Marie Eugenie Martin, he graduated from Arnaudville High School in 1934, Loyola Pharmacy School in 1938, and LSU Medical School in 1945. From 1945 to 1948, he served in the armed forces. He delivered most of his grandchildren and was the town doctor for Arnaudville. In 1939, he married Ruth Grace Wilbert (seated, left) and they had eight children (standing, from left to right): Dr. Robert II, Ruth "Sis" Grace, John Michael, Patrick Craig Sr., Harriet, Melissa, Victoria, and David.

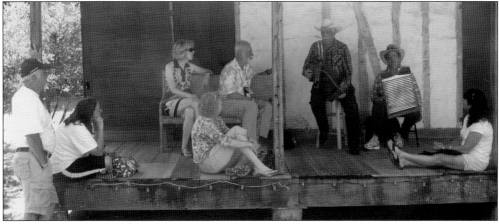

The City of Opelousas Tourist Information and Welcome Center is located on the grounds of Le Vieux Village, which was created in 1988 at the eastern entrance to Opelousas along Highway 190. The center houses the Jim Bowie display, sponsored by the Opelousas Kiwanis Club, in a house moved there from Grand Prairie. Bowie, an American hero of the 1836 Battle of the Alamo, once lived in Opelousas. A Creole Tour group is seen here on the porch of the Venus House, next door to the Jim Bowie exhibit. Goldman Thibodeaux is playing accordion and Theresa Thibodeaux is on *frottoir* (washboard).

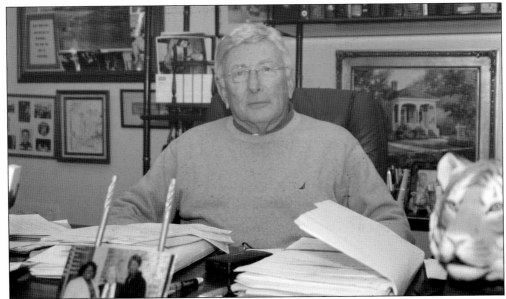

In 2012, Opelousas attorney Leslie J. Schiff, with the firm of Schiff, Scheckman & White, received the Louisiana State Bar Association Committee on the Profession's Professionalism Award. Schiff, who served as the Louisiana State Bar Association president in 1989–1990, received the award for his outstanding leadership in the creation and implementation of law school professionalism orientation programs. He is a frequent lecturer on ethics issues and a member of the LSU Law Center's board of trustees and chancellor's council.

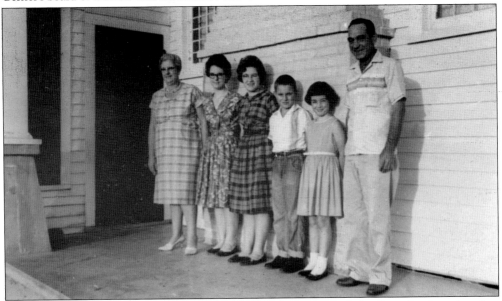

Historically, the citizenry of St. Landry Parish was predominately Catholic. Sacred and secular often intertwined, as the church's rituals were frequently the center of daily life. Public schools allowed students to receive religious instruction during school time. Seen here in 1960 are Wilhelmina (far left) and Earl Savoie Sr. (far right) with some of their children (from left to right): Lanell, Brenda, Earl Jr., and Darylin. This photograph was taken to commemorate the purchase of a new school bus by Earl Sr., a bus driver for the St. Landry Parish school system.

Vance Andrus, a native of Opelousas, was a founding partner of the Lafayette law firm of Andrus Boudreaux, which concentrates in mass tort litigation. Andrus received his bachelor of science degree from the University of Louisiana at Lafayette, where he received the Alumni Award as the outstanding graduating senior and served as the student government president of the College of Liberal Arts. He then attended law school at Louisiana State University and was a member of the Louisiana Law Review. He clerked for justice Albert Tate Jr. of the Louisiana Supreme Court. He is married to Colleen Houston and they currently reside in Conifer, Colorado.

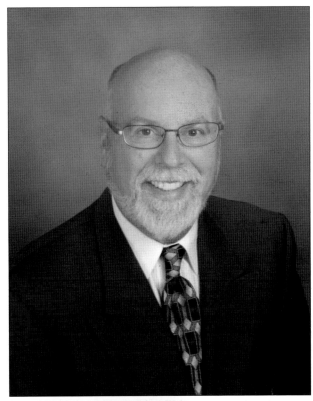

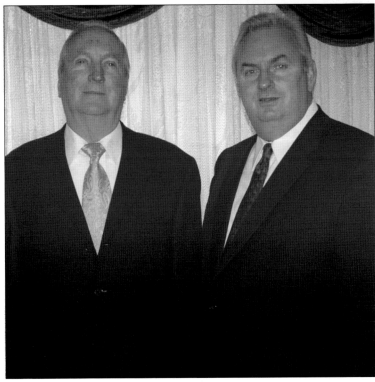

Marcus Ray Majors Sr. (left) came to the parish in 1957. He and his wife, Geneva Sanders Majors, raised their four children in Melville, where he served as pastor of the First Pentecostal Church for over 52 years. A St. Landry Parish resident since his birth on May 8, 1959, Marcus Ray "Mark" Majors Jr., and his wife, Ginger Travis Majors, also raised their four children in the Melville community. Their business developed emergency medical services for rural areas.

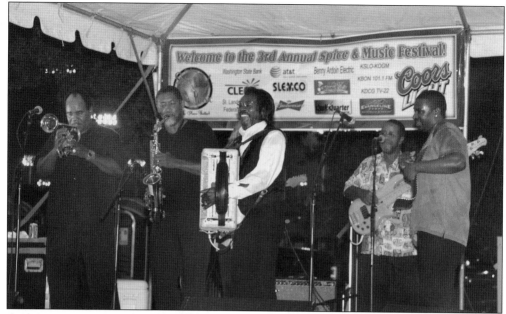

On May 14, 2012, the seventh annual Opelousas Spice & Music Festival was held in Opelousas. Mackenzie Ann Foreman of Cottonport, Louisiana, was crowned queen. Also crowned during the pageant were Emily Elizabeth Vidrine of Opelousas (Teen Miss Opelousas Spice and Music), Rebecca Richard (Lady Opelousas Spice and Music), and Claudia Marie Johnson Carrol (Ms. Opelousas Spice and Music). Here, on June 1, 2007, Buckwheat Zydeco and the Ils Sont Partis Band perform at the festival.

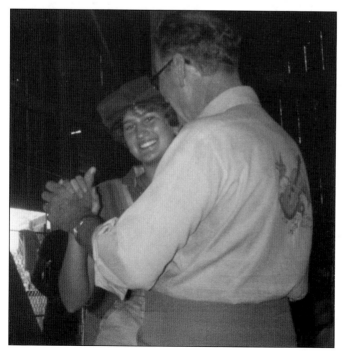

A blend of musical performances was held at the festival in 2012. Prominent Cajun fiddler Hadley J. Castille, a native of Pecaniere, near Leonville, and the recipient of many awards, including the American Folk Heritage Award, presented a fiddle workshop featuring an ensemble of female musicians, including Anya Schoenegge Burgess, Jane Vidrine, Gina Forsyth, Esther Tyree Mertz, and Sarah Jayde Williams. Accompanying the fiddlers on guitar was Christine Balfa, seen here in 1992 dancing with her father, Dewey Balfa, an iconic fiddler who contributed to the popularity of Cajun music.

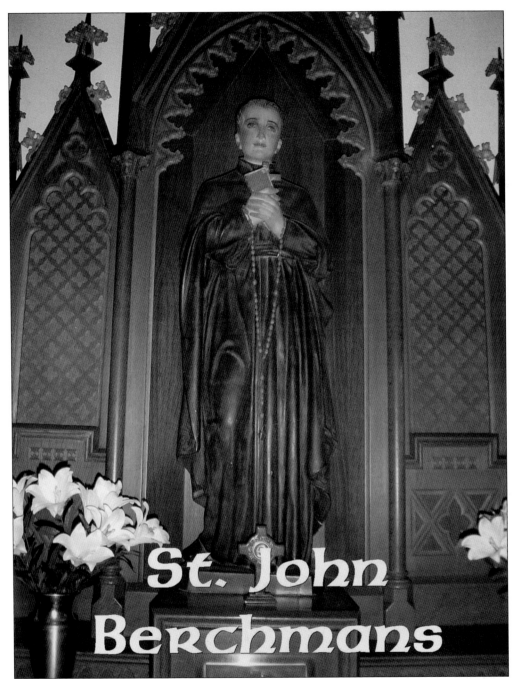

St. John Berchmans

St. John Berchmans was born in Belgium. In 1616, he was received into the novitiate; in 1621, he died at the age of 22. He was canonized in 1888. One of his three miracles required for canonization occurred at the Academy of the Sacred Heart in Grand Coteau. In 1867, Berchmans twice appeared to a postulate Mary Wilson and cured her of cancer on her deathbed. The shrine to Berchmans seen here is the only shrine at the exact location of a confirmed miracle in the United States. When the Academy opened a boys' division in 2006, it was named St. John Berchmans School. It includes a small chapel honoring him.

DISCOVER THOUSANDS OF LOCAL HISTORY BOOKS
FEATURING MILLIONS OF VINTAGE IMAGES

Arcadia Publishing, the leading local history publisher in the United States, is committed to making history accessible and meaningful through publishing books that celebrate and preserve the heritage of America's people and places.

Find more books like this at
www.arcadiapublishing.com

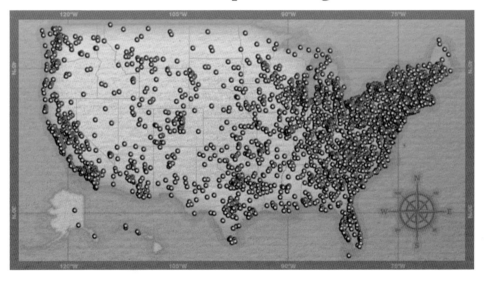

Search for your hometown history, your old stomping grounds, and even your favorite sports team.

Consistent with our mission to preserve history on a local level, this book was printed in South Carolina on American-made paper and manufactured entirely in the United States. Products carrying the accredited Forest Stewardship Council (FSC) label are printed on 100 percent FSC-certified paper.

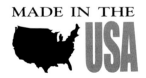